AF386636

GHOST
GIRL

GHOST GIRL

Surviving the
Black Swan Murder Trial

A MEMOIR

EVA BENEFIELD

GALLERY BOOKS UK

London · New York · Amsterdam/Antwerp · Sydney/Melbourne · Toronto · New Delhi

First published in the United States by Gallery Books,
an imprint of Simon & Schuster, LLC, 2026

First published in Great Britain by Simon & Schuster UK Ltd, 2026

Copyright © Eva Benefield, 2026

The right of Eva Benefield to be identified as the author of this work has been
asserted in accordance with the Copyright, Designs and Patents Act, 1988.

1 3 5 7 9 10 8 6 4 2

Simon & Schuster UK Ltd
7th Floor
199 Bishopsgate
London EC2M 3TY

For more than 100 years, Simon & Schuster has championed authors and the
stories they create. By respecting the copyright of an author's intellectual property, you
enable Simon & Schuster and the author to continue publishing exceptional books for
years to come. We thank you for supporting the author's copyright by purchasing an
authorized edition of this book.

No amount of this book may be reproduced or stored in any format, nor may it be
uploaded to any website, database, language-learning model, or other repository, retrieval,
or artificial intelligence system without express permission. All rights reserved. Inquiries
may be directed to Simon & Schuster, 199 Bishopsgate, London EC2M 3TY or
RightsMailbox@simonandschuster.co.uk

Simon & Schuster strongly believes in freedom of expression and stands against
censorship in all its forms. For more information, visit BooksBelong.com.

www.simonandschuster.co.uk
www.simonandschuster.com.au
www.simonandschuster.co.in

Simon & Schuster Australia, Sydney
Simon & Schuster India, New Delhi

The authorised representative in the EEA is Simon & Schuster Netherlands BV,
Herculesplein 96, 3584 AA Utrecht, Netherlands. info@simonandschuster.nl

Some names and identifying details have been changed.

The author and publishers have made all reasonable efforts to contact copyright-holders
for permission, and apologise for any omissions or errors in the form of credits given.
Corrections may be made to future printings.

A CIP catalogue record for this book is available from the British Library

Hardback ISBN: 978-1-3985-6009-3
Trade Paperback ISBN: 978-1-3985-6010-9
eBook ISBN: 978-1-3985-6011-6

Interior design by Jaime Putorti

Printed and Bound in the UK using 100% Renewable Electricity at CPI Group (UK) Ltd

To my mom,
who taught me that words matter, so choose them wisely.

And to my dad,
who taught me that everything comes right in the end.

CONTENTS

GHOST
GIRL

DEAD DAD JOKES

When I was nineteen, my dad was shot and killed by his swimsuit model/ballerina bride, who was thirty years his junior and the craziest psycho bitch in the microgreens aisle at Whole Foods. Fact.

Soon, the bottom-feeders were everywhere. I was awash in tabloid gore. One minute, I was a normal freshman at the College of Charleston studying art, and the next minute, I was a circus freak. *20/20, 48 Hours, Access Hollywood, Court TV, TMZ,* you name it—they were at my front door with a camera guy, and a boom guy, and some glowed-up producer in search of a fresh angle on the same old yarn.

Everybody was like, *What's the punch line, Eva? What's the lesson learned? How do you feel about your stepmom shooting your dad? Are you doing okay now, honey? What comes next for you? Did you actually make a joke about your dad getting murdered on TikTok? Do you really think that's funny?*

I think dark humor is my way of coping. But some people get triggered. The serious adult world isn't ready for my dead dad jokes. They don't understand that it's my way of coping with the inevitable PTSD after such things. Plus, what happened was so absurd, so banal and terrible, and so completely avoidable that you just have to laugh sometimes. That doesn't mean it's not painful. I make jokes because it *is* painful.

Being inside an infamous true crime story isn't like how you think it would be. These things don't add up in forty-eight minutes minus commercial interruptions. It's not like it looks on TV. They don't show you the quiet parts that you can't say out loud. Like, for one thing, it's isolating. People can't relate to you. They don't know what to say. Not my friends or their parents or even my boyfriend. I had to break up with him after three and a half years because he kept telling me to get over myself.

I can't blame him, really. He's right; I should get over myself. What I'm going through is almost too much, even for me, and I'm used to it. The whole thing can be so stupid and cringe. There is nothing anybody can say that will change anything anyway. It just is what it is sometimes, and people have a hard time with that, when they can't say or do anything to alter the facts. Me? I look for the jokes.

We all have a choice about how we respond to loss or injustice or just plain old garden-variety stupidity. Losing both my parents like I did was incredibly hard, but it's all hard. Growing up is hard, going to work is hard, getting out of bed and getting ready for the day is particularly hard. I slept through jury duty last week.

I think waking up in the morning is the worst time of the day for me, because my dad used to cook me breakfast. The Low Country has taught me that there's no use pretending things are easier than they are. There will come a time when you have to crack the shell if you want to get to what's inside. And that always takes some doing. Even the stuff you thought you could count on to be easy, like being a kid, is hard. Honestly, I think older people forget that, and they shouldn't. It's hard to be young, and it's hard to stay young when there are so many adult problems to cope with.

It's hard to make mistakes, lose myself, then find myself again when everybody is watching and wondering if I'm going to crash and burn or crack up quietly in the corner. Only I don't. Instead, I'm doing okay. I think people find my strength disturbing, and that's hard, too. I keep waiting to implode like everybody expects me to. I think it would put everybody's mind at ease if I did. Only I can't. I don't. That's not how this feels. I feel strangely liberated. I mean, the worst has already happened to me . . . twice. Who's gonna stop me now? I'm a racing car passing by like Lady Godiva.

I do get anxious sometimes. A lot of times. I try to remind myself that you can't die of a panic attack, even though you think you're gonna drop over dead right there on the sand while it's happening. I have yet to see anyone actually die right in front of me—I mean, except for that deer my boyfriend Pete hit by accident down the Old Fall Line Road. You can't freak out about it. These are the kinds of things that are bound to happen on dark country lanes at night. That's just how it is down here. In Charleston, life and death live right next door to each other and have for centuries.

Existential threats are floating like icebergs all over the place these days, not just in my life. The force of the undertow is pulling us all out into the deep, frigid ocean. I thought it might be helpful for people to hear directly from somebody who's been through the worst that we are tougher than we think we are. We can survive just about anything if we put our minds to it and stay positive. It sounds trite, I know, but it's more difficult than you think. Still, it can be done. We can choose to remain optimistic. We can navigate past the fractured ice.

I want people to know, and especially girls like me, that no matter where you are in life, or what you're facing, small or large, it's all important, and you're not alone. Somebody else is going through the same thing you are. Probably experiencing a lot of the very same emotions at exactly the same time. And it's okay to talk or even joke about it. There's awesome power hidden inside your vulnerability. Like a smooth black pearl in the hollow of a dull gray oyster. It's your buried treasure. It's important to share these precious secrets with somebody you trust. To tell them the truth about how you really feel. To me, that is the definition of strength and resilience.

I say we have a choice, but that's not completely true. You don't have a choice about a lot of stuff, especially when you're a girl. The things that changed my life were not my choices. They were other people's decisions, people who really should have known better. But now, my dad is gone, and I have a choice of my own to make. It can be weird telling the truth in a world full of lies. But somebody has to stand up for the facts, and that somebody may as well be me. Because I've stared cold reality in the face and what I saw doesn't fit on an Instagram tile. That's why I'm writing this book.

It was a little like this—I'm a surfer. It's Charleston, so we don't get the big waves, but they're big enough to turn you upside down and sideways when conditions are just right. So, imagine you're in the shallows. And then you see a wave, way out at sea. From where you're standing, it looks like just a little white froth on the surface of the water. A friendly whitecap that wouldn't hurt anybody. By the time you realize you're dealing with a freak monster wave that is going to toss you around like a rag doll, it's already too late. It's already on top of you, and you have to go under it, or get on top of it, or figure out how to hold your breath and dive right through, because there's just no getting around the facts. One way or another, that swell is going to crash according to its own physics. It's going to do what it does, no matter how you feel about it.

Girls like me, we live on the fall line, where solid ground meets the Precambrian muck and lazy rivers gather power, rushing down into the Low Country, carving rapids and water-falls into the solid bedrock. We know how to wade knee-deep without falling. We aren't afraid of white water, or sharks, or riptides, or the undertow. We know when to duck under, when to rise up, and how to ride the crest of our wave to shore, no matter what anybody else has to say about it, no matter who we leave in our wake. That's what I learned in the Low Country. And that's what I want to share with other girls like me, because we are the strongest substance on the planet, and the truth's last, best hope.

CHAPTER 1

THE LOW COUNTRY

Growing up in the Low Country, I spent most of my time with both feet in the water. My father tried to teach me a healthy respect for the sea, or at least to be careful, but it was a nonstarter. I am not careful. Even now, when you'd think I would have learned my lesson. My dad was a navy pilot. He landed fighter jets on aircraft carriers under cover of darkness on stormy seas. Did he really think he was going to raise a hesitant child?

My dad was more careful than I was, now that I think about it. Until he wasn't at all. I could tell my dad had seen some things out on the open water that he didn't want to remember or talk about. He loved the beach, but he was always a little afraid of the ocean. Me? I am water. I have a hard time knowing where I stop and the sea begins. And back then, standing in the shallows, holding my dad's hand, I wasn't afraid of anything.

"The sea can be tricky, Eva. She's an unpredictable force. You have to respect that," my dad would say like he was some salty old fisherman. He'd look at me then, his twinkling blue eyes searching mine for a spark of recognition, to see that his warning was landing. But I was a feckless, savage child. I get it from him. He knew that no matter what he said, I'd dive right in. Laughing in the face of disaster is straight up Benefield.

"You just never know what can happen out there, Eva. The ocean can change on a dime, and she's not going to send you a memo beforehand." He'd put his index finger up like he was testing the direction of the wind and gaze out over the water with his ten-mile stare. "You have to be ready, and the only way to be ready is to be careful." It's almost ironic now when I think about what happened next. I loved my dad more than anybody else on the planet, and I listened to him most of the time. But I just didn't get how you can be ready for something you don't even know is coming. How do you prepare for the unknown unknown? I don't know, and obviously, neither did he.

Before everything changed, I was a normal, happy kid growing up in a normal, happy family in a normal, happy house in a normal, happy neighborhood. Nothing bad had ever happened to me. I was wrapped in the beautiful blanket of my illusion of invulnerability. I thought of the ocean as kind, even when it was angry. Like a mom who you know loves you, and who is going to support you when you're down, but who will also kick your butt when you deserve it. I understood that the sea could be dangerous, but it was mine. My ocean. My Low Country. My beach. My mother.

Now I know the truth. Nothing is mine but me.

When I was first learning to surf in the shallows, I could sometimes feel the sandpapery skin of a shark brushing past my legs. Once, I saw a fin pop up right in front of me, and I wasn't even scared. I don't know why. I probably should have been. But I figured the shark was a creature of the water, just like me. We had something vast and fundamental in common. We didn't have to trifle with one another. We could peacefully coexist.

I go beachcombing for shark's teeth sometimes. I keep them in a jar. There are soft hollows in the muddy bottoms out past the shrimp docks, and if you feel around with your feet, you can always find a bunch. I like the way a shark's tooth feels in my hand, cold and smooth and hard as obsidian. They are literally all over the place down here if you know where to look. Shark's teeth have no roots, so they fall out all the time. It's not a big deal. The sharks just grow new ones. Your average shark can go through fifty thousand teeth in her lifetime. Nature is so sick.

I'm borderline tomboy, I guess you could say. Despite my being a slave to fashion and my almost religious devotion to weekly mani-pedis. That's my mom in me. I'm never satisfied with how I look. Last month, I got bangs. Before that, I got a new tattoo that I drew myself. It's a tiny beach umbrella on a tiny beach, with a tiny stick figure man sitting in a beach chair like my dad used to do. Yesterday, I pierced my nose. Next month, I'm piercing my nipples. Maybe.

I'm my dad's only child. My mom had me, and then my dad had a vasectomy, so I was the end of the line, until I wasn't.

My dad taught me the same things he would have taught me if I had been born a boy. I grew up hunting and fishing the Low Country since I was almost big enough to hold a rod or a gun without falling over. I'm still almost big enough. I'm tiny and compact, like my dad. I loved going out on the boat fishing or crabbing the flats at low tide, just my dad and me. He couldn't really surf anymore, because of a back injury he got in the war, but he'd paddle out and watch me catch my wave. We were close.

There's something thrilling about crossing over the fall line into a place where the solid ground gives way to fluvial gunk deposited there over sixty-five million years ago. The rivers that have wandered all the way from the Blue Ridge Mountains eastward and then south to the Carolinas finally hit the fall line and turn into white water, leaping and bubbling the rest of their way to the sea. It's exhilarating to watch something rush so joyfully and forcefully back to its source.

From the time I could walk and talk, I loved this land and the people who live here. Fishing boats and fishermen and quiet, deep water; sun-bleached shells, and shrimp and grits and tomato pies in baskets handwoven out of sweetgrass by the Gullah women. Porches with their ceilings painted haint blue to ward off the ghosts that haunt the thresholds down here. The acrid pinch of the pluff mud in my nostrils smells like home to me. I'm as at ease on the water as I am on land, really. Most of us who grew up in Charleston are like that. We are all creatures of the Low Country, as much as the minnows and fiddler crabs and the white herons are.

At high tide, you can see the fish moving through the marsh looking for pogies. If it's a flood tide, the serious fishermen are out trying to catch a prize-winning redfish while the wind whips up the fronds of the giant palmettos, making ripples across the whole bayou. It looks like something from another millennium. Ancient and primeval. Every hungry creature finds a meal in the marsh, and I love it in all its carnivorous glory. Only now, I fish alone.

My dad always traveled a lot on business. He worked for a start-up that was developing new technology for the government. When he was in town, though, he was the one who got me up and ready for school. We'd have breakfast together, then he'd drop me off at school on his way to work. My house was a warm, loving, and comfortable place, where everybody gathered around the holidays, for sure, but also just anytime. My mom was an excellent homemaker and hostess. She was not a great cook. That was my dad's department. My nanna owned a bed-and-breakfast where my dad grew up. My dad was a Texas cowboy by way of the fat and savory breakfast kitchens of Huntsville, Alabama, so he knew his way around a basted egg, that's for damn sure.

"I know how to rattle those pots and pans, so get out of my way, women!" he'd say. My mom and I would roll our eyes. Then he'd crack two eggs into the pan and flip them over without breaking the yolks and slide them onto my plate. Then he would whisk up some egg whites for my mom, who was always counting her calories. She lived mostly on egg whites, coffee, and green shakes. I come from a very coffee-friendly family. To this day, I pretty much live on Americanos, blueberries, broccoli, avocados, and eggs sunny-side up. I like food, at least, to be simple and straightforward.

When I was born, my oldest half brother, Ben, was already a teenager. He went off to college when I was like three years old. But he was close to our mom, so he came home a lot. He would bring all his football teammates with him, and they would all sleep over like a big, sloppy frat boy slumber party. Those were fun times. Ben was never too sure about my dad. They weren't close. I mean, my brothers had a dad of their own, and Marty was still very involved in their lives. Ben sure loved my dad's cooking, though. My dad and I would pick up food for everyone at Whole Foods on Friday afternoon, and then my dad would bake his famous oatmeal cookies, and those boys would toss those heifers down before they even cooled off.

My other half brother, John, who is eight years older than I am, was around the house a little longer. I was twelve when John went off to school, and Ben went off to war that same year. Then it was just my parents and me, and things changed. It got quieter around the house. My life became very routine. Wake up, eat breakfast, go to school, leave school, complain about school, play outside with my friends, eat dinner, go to bed, wake up too early, complain about waking up too early, go to school, complain about school, rinse and repeat.

During the summer, we went to the beach all the time. My mom would pack sandwiches, and she and my dad would sit under the umbrella and watch me make drip castles on the shoreline. On the weekends, I'd "help" my dad work on his latest home improvement project. He was always working on something around our house, and there were always about five projects in process at any given time. Few if any of his installations ever got finished. But he was determined, and he was always busy doing something for us.

Every Saturday morning, my dad would discover that he needed a nail, or a drill bit, or just anything he could think of so we had an excuse to pop out to Home Depot. He'd go looking for his stuff while I got lost in the art supply aisle. My dad taught me how to draw, so he never pushed back on art supplies. I could get whatever I wanted. That art supply aisle at Home Depot was like my candy store. I think we spent more time at the Home Depot than actually fixing anything, which is probably why I don't remember our dishwasher working or the water in the master bath ever being hot. But we didn't care. We were always a work in progress, and we liked it that way.

My mom was high-key. She started crying at the drop of a hat, I swear, which used to drive me crazy. It was so uncomfortable. We'd be in like the grocery store, or a parking lot, or a gas station, and she'd just cut loose with the waterworks. Once, she spilled coffee in my brother's new car, which had a white interior. She literally cried for an hour while my brother tried to comfort her. She never wanted to cause a commotion, but when she discovered that she had, she'd dissolve into a puddle of tears and cause a commotion all over again. Then we'd all reassure her it was going to be okay and that we weren't mad at her, not even a little bit. I was more like my dad, the navy pilot who could land on a postage stamp in rough seas. We were stoic—low-key Low Country warriors.

On Wednesday, December 2, 2015, my dad was on the road, so my mom stepped up and made me a green shake for breakfast. She always had a green shake in her hand or was shoving one into mine. My mom was passionate about certain things. She felt deeply and often. It was like her nerves traveled right up close to the surface. I could almost see her emotions circulating, blue and fragile beneath her translucent skin.

I can be a little grouchy when I first wake up. That day, the Eva forecast was cloudy with a chance of severe thunderstorms and maybe even a little hail if people didn't watch themselves. I barely spoke to my mom while she blended breakfast. We had gotten into yet another stupid and boring argument about how or when or if I did my homework. For some reason, this made me furious. I can't quite remember now, but I either had done my homework or had good reasons for not doing my homework. Whatever it was, I was right, she was wrong, and it was half past draw the line.

I was stomping around the house and then dragging my feet to make sure I made us both late. Well, I was a teenage girl, and I was morally outraged. In the face of injustice, teen girls will go to the mattresses, and there will be no dealing with us after that. The negotiate-by date will have expired. There will be an unavoidable escalation of hostilities.

My mom tried to talk to me like nothing was wrong on the way to school, but I wasn't having it. I closed up tight as a clam. She didn't take it personally, which was another nice thing about my mom. She got that I was a teenager. She took things as they came with me. She didn't get bent out of shape. She didn't expect me to be somebody I wasn't. She took mercy on me and didn't force me to go through cotillion. She said I could learn what fork to use just as well sitting at her table without going to some stupid society school. My mom had what I now think of as grace.

We pulled into the pickup area of my school late. My feet-dragging strategy had worked perfectly, but I don't know why I had chosen this tactic. My mom was notoriously and chronically and unapologetically late. She had no problem being tardy. My dad used to joke that she would be late to her own wedding, and I think she legit was. I'm the one who was punctual to a fault. And now I was the one who was uncomfortable walking into class ten minutes past the bell. I had punished myself. I do that sometimes. My mom used to say, "Eva, you will cut off your nose to spite your face," and she was dead-on right about that.

My mom told me to have a good day at school and said she loved me. She told me that all the time, so I barely listened. I slammed the car door in her face and told her I hated her. I know, nice, right? Okay, so I wasn't winning any Daughter of the Year awards that day, but I was trying to make a point, and I was 1,000 percent convinced of the justice of my cause. I wasn't giving my mom an inch.

Of course, I had forgotten about the whole thing the second I hit homeroom. My friend Vanessa, old Mr. Alex Dunleavy's granddaughter, told me that morning that I could apply for a job at their family's restaurant for the summer. I was over the moon about it, because it meant I could go surfing every day on Sullivan's without having to ask anybody for a ride. Dunleavy's Pub was a cute little place on the corner of Middle Street and Station 22½ on Sullivan's Island, only my very favorite place on the whole planet.

My parents have a plaque on the wall at Dunleavy's because that is technically where they met after a long day on the beach way back in 1999, when the only thing on Station 22½ was Dunleavy's and the old signal cannon. A lot of my favorite memories were made in that little green storefront, where the walls are covered in street signs and license plates and pictures of people wearing Dunleavy's T-shirts going back to, like, the Jurassic Period. Plus, they have the best grilled wings you will ever taste in your life, and that's not trivial.

I remember I texted my folks about the possible job the second homeroom let out. I didn't think twice about it when my dad texted back, but my mom didn't respond. I figured she was probably off somewhere doing something important. Plus, my mom was not much of a texter and was notoriously bad about checking her messages. She got very immersed in her life. I liked that about her. Whether it was working with a kid who needed speech therapy or hanging with her ladies' prayer group, she was present. She inhabited her life fully, and she expected me to do the same.

Then at the end of the day, she'd ask me all about wins and make too much of a fuss over every dumb little accomplishment. I appreciated that she expected me to live my own life.

She didn't bug me all the time, like a lot of my friends' moms did to them. My mom trusted me to make good choices for myself. Meanwhile, sometimes I did, sometimes I didn't, but I think she knew that was the only way I was gonna learn. Her philosophy of parenting was that you can only tell a kid so many things, then they have to learn it for themselves the hard way. And she let me do that. Which was cool of her. Came in handy down the line.

After school, I ran to the pickup area, determined to prosecute my case one more time. I tried to work myself back up into a huff about the homework, but it was pointless. I was too excited to tell her about the Dunleavy's opportunity. I got to the pickup area, and my mom wasn't there, but that didn't mean much. I always allowed her an extra half hour before I started to worry. My dad taught me growing up that being even one second late could make the difference between a successful mission and a full-on disaster. He really put an emphasis on punctuality, so I got used to showing up early, just to make double sure. My mom, not so much. These days, I'm never on time. After everything that's happened, I mean, seriously, what's the point? I know. Poor attitude. I'm working on that.

After thirty minutes, I dialed my mom, but big surprise, she didn't pick up. Then I texted her. More crickets. Most of the other kids had already left the parking area by then, and I started thinking maybe I should come up with a plan B, just in case her car broke down or something, which happened sometimes. She never got her oil checked. My dad was on the road, so I couldn't call him. I saw this girl Parker who I hadn't seen since elementary school, still waiting for her ride.

I wandered over, trying to look casual, and was like, "Hey, Parker, do you think your mom would mind giving me a lift home since my mom seems to be MIA, and oh, by the way, how are you doing? It's been a minute, right?" So awkward. Parker was cool, though.

"No problem at all. I'm sure my mom won't mind," she said, and smiled in a way that made it seem like she thought I needed a hug. Did I need a hug? Maybe I did. When her mom pulled up and we hopped in, I felt instantly and almost indescribably relieved. It was only after I had relaxed for a second that I even noticed I was so anxious.

I didn't want to say anything, because I didn't want to let myself get carried away, and I didn't want to be messy in front of Parker and her mom for no reason, or for like any reason. But I was starting to feel a little panicky about my mom not showing up or answering her phone or even texting back about the job at Dunleavy's. I mean, where was she? Was she still pissed at me about the homework thing? Was she trying to make a point? Did she want me to remember that I still needed her to make me breakfast or pick me up at school, or whatever, so maybe I should be a little nicer? She was right. I acted like a brat. I should be nicer to my mom.

We pulled up to the front of my house, and all the lights were off. My mom's car was in the driveway, which was weird. I mean, if she wasn't in her car, then where was she? Maybe she went for a run. Maybe she thought somebody else was giving me a ride. Maybe she and her BFF, Melanie, were hanging and lost track of time. The house being dark wasn't unusual. My mom loved natural light, so even though our house was in the woods and sunlight was in short supply, she made my dad uninstall every single overhead fixture in our house. Then she brought the natural light in with a neutral palette and soft petal-pink accents. I like that my mom felt strongly about things like natural light and plant-forward meals and keeping a cute home. I like that she had a strong faith in God and in nature, in green shakes, and in me.

I walked up to my front door, and it was locked. I knocked . . . Nope. I walked around and tried our side door . . . also locked. Maybe my mom was sleeping. She had been up late the night before organizing her winter clothes. Maybe she was taking a nap. I wasn't sure what to do at that point. I called my dad, and it went straight to voicemail. I didn't want to leave a message. I mean, what would I say? The sky is blue, and Mom is late? Parker's mom suggested we go get dinner and try again a little later. We got back in the car and went to the nearest Chick-fil-A. I wasn't hungry, and I am always hungry. I was suppressing a scream in my head. My Chick-fil-A tasted like ass.

After dinner, we headed back to my house. By then, I was practically holding my breath, hoping a light would be on or that something, anything, would have changed. As we pulled up, though, I could see the house was still dark. Everything was exactly the same as when we left it. Parker's mom told me she'd wait until I got inside, so I went and banged on the front door, but there was still no answer. The panic set in so hard then I could taste the fear on my tongue. It tasted like tin.

Parker and her mom pulled into our driveway and got out of the car. I was crawling through the bushes in front of my house so I could peek through my parents' bedroom windows and see if my mom was sleeping. I saw my mom's silhouette lying on the bed as if she were taking a nap, but when I tapped on the window, she didn't wake up or move or open her eyes, or anything. At some point right around then, I switched on my autopilot and emotionally checked out.

Parker's mom went across the street and got my neighbor Mr. Wilson to help me get into the house. Mr. Wilson, Melanie's husband and my dad's main fishing buddy, came over and investigated the situation. Mr. Wilson told me to stand back, and then, *boom*, he broke down the front door. I don't even remember how he managed to do that, but before I knew it, the doorframe was in splinters. My dad tried to fix the doorframe for years afterward, but no matter what he did, that crack stayed right where it was. Like a fall line dividing before and after. Mr. Wilson went inside to check on my mom, while Parker and her mom and I sat in rocking chairs on the porch without saying much. Mr. Wilson was only inside for a couple of seconds, and then he came out on the porch and looked at me.

"I'm sorry, Eva, but you're going to have to come in and grab Sully," he said. "He's guarding your mom and almost bit my hand off when I tried to get close." He looked at me, his eyes wide and round. I stood up, but felt a little faint and sat right back down. Then Mr. Wilson gave me his hand, and together, we went into the house so I could grab Sully.

This would be a good time to introduce you to the love of my life and the all-around greatest dog that ever lived, my golden retriever Sully. I picked him out of the litter the summer before seventh grade. He is the sweetest, happiest, sloppiest dog ever. He chases his tail when he gets excited, and he just loves everyone to pieces. He goes everywhere with me, and everywhere we go, everybody loves on him, and he loves it, which is why I love him so much. Sully is pure love. This is how I knew something serious was happening. Sully had never growled at anybody in his whole life. Sully is a people person.

I walked into the house and into my parents' bedroom. I saw my mom's boots in the doorway where she had kicked them off. I saw Sully, who saw me and wagged his tail once and put his head down, looking pathetic. Then I saw my mom, who was slouched halfway on the bed and halfway on the floor in a very unnatural-looking position. I didn't want to see any more after that. I called Sully, and he came to me right away. I pulled him outside onto the porch and sat back down in the rocking chair, stroking his ears and letting my mind go blank while Mr. Wilson went into the bedroom to help my mom.

I remember everyone around me talking and talking and saying things to one another and to me. You know, winter is on the way, it's getting cooler in the evenings now, or Eva, starting high school already, where does the time go? I don't know, I couldn't really make sense out of much. I was sealed off under my bell jar, deep in the drone zone, which is not a bad place to be when all hell breaks loose. Mr. Wilson came back out of the house after a few minutes. He looked at me and shook his head. That's when I knew for sure that I had lost my mom.

Mr. Wilson called the police and the paramedics, and then he called my dad. Melanie came across the street and brought me into their house while Mr. Wilson waited for emergency services. I was grateful for that. I didn't want to watch my mom's lifeless body get wheeled out on a stretcher with a white sheet over her face, or in a body bag like you see on *Law & Order*.

"I'm so sorry, sweetie. Can I make you some tea or something while you wait? Can I call anybody for you?" Melanie asked. She was my mom's best friend in Charleston, and I'm sure she must have been super upset also, but she never showed it to me. She was just calm and soothing and mom-ish. I've never thanked her for that, but I should.

"No, I'm fine, Mrs. Wilson, but thank you so kindly." It's one of the last things you hold on to in Charleston. Even when everything else has gone out from under you, you still have to be polite.

"Call me *Melanie*, honey. We're practically family," Mrs. Wilson said, and pulled a chair out for me at the kitchen table, and pushed me down into it, then rubbed my back softly with her perfect French tips. "Henry, will you make us some tea, please, darlin'?" Mrs. Wilson made a face at her son, Henry, who got up grudgingly, but out of respect for my situation did not roll his eyes like I knew he wanted to, and made us tea without too much of an attitude.

Henry was a prodigy pianist, and he practiced Mozart every morning while I got dressed for school, so I knew he wasn't a total caveman. Still, even prodigy piano boys down here can go for months without putting more than three words together. Henry plopped the steaming mug down in front of me, and Melanie pushed the honey pot toward me and then poured a shot of bourbon into my tea. "Go on," she said. "Drink your tea now, sweetie. You'll feel better. Don't tell your daddy, though. This will be our little secret." Then Henry and Melanie and I sat silently at the table, sipping tea, while the red and blue lights flashed across the white walls of their front room. The hot bourbon felt like a warm blanket on the inside.

It's so weird the stuff you talk about when tragedy visits. You talk about the same annoying random stuff you talked about before, except now it has a totally different feeling. The weather, the price of gas, a summer job, all the normal jibber jabber suddenly seems precious and sweet because of the very same things that used to drive you up a wall. The small talk reminds you of when things were routine and normal, which is reassuring when you think nothing will ever be normal again. Like when you find out your mom's dead and you can't shed a single tear.

Somebody called my sister-in-law Beverly to come get Sully and me and take us to Bev and Ben's house until my dad got a flight back home. Bev and I didn't talk much on the way, or like at all, really. That was kind of a relief, to tell you the truth. I was with family. I didn't have to say anything if I didn't want to. In a situation like that, what is there to say?

Looking back, I think Bev and I were both in shock. In the moment, though, I didn't know that. I'd never been in shock before. I didn't know what I was feeling except a huge relief to be quiet and have someone that loved me pick me up and take me home. As soon as I got inside, I took off my shoes, collapsed on the couch, pulled out my schoolbag, and, for the first time ever, did my homework without my mom yelling at me to quit goofing around and get to work.

CHAPTER 2

THE GHOSTS ENTER THE CHAT

I fell asleep halfway through my book report on *Lord of the Flies*, and Bev woke me up a couple of hours later and pushed Sully and me upstairs to lie down in their guest room. I fell back asleep in like two seconds flat, while Sully breathed dog snot and puppy love into the crook of my neck. My dad woke me up just before dawn. I remember thinking, *Oh, thank God, the eagle has landed.*

"Eva, are you awake?" he whispered, stroking my hair like he used to when I was little and was having a bad dream.

"Now I am," I said, sitting up and rubbing my eyes. I felt hungover from the grief and the shock of it all.

"I'm sorry I woke you, honey, but I wanted to talk to you right away. I'm so sorry about your mom, baby. I'm so sorry I wasn't here."

"That's okay," I said, because I mean, what else could I say? I didn't blame him for anything. None of this was anybody's fault. That part was hard, too, having nobody to blame. Just random happenstance, and now you have to live with the fall-out. It just is what it is. That part really sucked.

"You know, I've dealt with death a lot in my life from the time I was young, the same age that you are now." His words caught in his throat, so I didn't say anything. I just waited for him to collect himself. I knew that if he started bawling, I'd start bawling, and I knew that neither one of us was ready for that. So, I just waited to see what was going to happen next. Sometimes, you need your father to take the wheel.

I knew that my dad had lost his own father when he was fifteen. He knew better than anybody, probably even more than I did, about how I was feeling right then. I was still completely clueless about what I was or was not feeling. I needed to hear from him, to understand how he felt I should feel about this. I wasn't used to this sensation. This was a new and uncomfortable sensation for a fourteen-year-old who was intent on becoming her own person. Needing my dad to tell me how to feel was not on my bingo card. But right then, I was hanging on his every word.

"I'm so sorry that you lost your mom," he said finally. "I would have given anything to protect you from having to face this kind of loss. I know how much you loved your mom, how much you still need her. You're way too young to have to cope with this."

"It's okay," I said again, even though it so totally was not. "It's not your fault, Dad."

"I know, it's nobody's fault, honey, but that doesn't make it okay, and it doesn't make it fair." My dad squeezed my hand

and got a faraway look in his eyes. "In the navy, Eva, I lost some good friends, great guys who were working right there next to me day after day for months. Some for years. These were the people I trusted with my life. One minute, they were there, and the next, they were gone. But I wasn't gone. I was still standing there. That's the part that always bothered me, how unfair that was. How random and senseless. But I don't want that to bother you. You have a right to live your life just the way you want to live it. And I don't want you to ever feel guilty about being a survivor."

I looked up at my dad then, and he looked adrift, lost in another place and time. I wondered for a sec if he remembered he was talking to me, or if he was out on the fall line, talking to ghosts. Then Sully sneezed and brought us all back from the sweet hereafter.

"Now we're going to go through the grieving process, Eva, you and me together. It's going to be hard, and sometimes you're going to feel like you'll always feel as sad as you feel right now. But you won't. It will get better. And for as long as it lasts, we'll have each other, and that will really help. I'm going to be right here with you, every step of the way, baby." My dad smiled sadly, wiped a couple of tears from his cheek, and held me close for longer than either of us was comfortable with. But for the first time since my mom died, I felt a little better.

"Are you going to get remarried?" I asked him, my face still pressed into his chest. "Like, are you going to want to start a new family?" I pulled away, wiped my snot on my sleeve, and searched his true-blue eyes for reassurance. I don't know why I asked him this right then. I have a sixth sense that kicks in at seriously the worst times.

"That's never going to happen, Eva," my dad said. "Don't give that a second thought."

I believed him, because my dad always told me the truth.

But of course, it was all a big fat lie.

CHAPTER 3

PAPERWHITES ARE
THE FRIENDLIEST FLOWER

I say that I'm from Charleston, but like a lot of folks who say they're from Charleston, I technically grew up in Mount Pleasant. We had a cute house in a cute neighborhood, not fancy like the Old Village, but well-kept, aspirational lawns and flower beds that bloomed in harmony with the seasons. In spring, magnolias and wisteria, and then in deep summer, crepe myrtle and camellias, azaleas and jasmine and blue hydrangeas. My neighborhood was leafy and sweet, and my house was made of bricks, so the Big Bad Wolf was never gonna blow it down.

My dad built me a tree house in the backyard when I was two. I drove by the other day, and it's still there. It's funny the things that remain. I think about my mom every time I blend a shake, or see a paperwhite, or book a nail appointment, or look in the mirror. I think about my dad every time I breathe. "So charming, Renee," people always said to my mom when they'd come over for dinner for the first time. "So cozy and quaint," which is Southern for *small and needing some work*, but we were in the right school district, and the house had good bones.

When I drive by today, the house looks finished at long last. All the ends tied up tastefully, like a beautiful birthday bow. And I don't think it looks nearly as nice as it did back then, when all the ends were still loose and young and unconcerned about appearances. That's Southern for *irony*.

Mount Pleasant is across the bridge from Charleston, just on the other side of the Cooper River. It feels suburban, but we act like we've all been there since Fort Sumter fired its first fuck-you. We're clannish and tribal, rural in a way that only the Low Country can produce. Even though we are only a twenty-minute ride from downtown Charleston, we all still have a co-lonial patina dating all the way back to 1683, if you scratch below the surface of things. As is the case with many of the charming suburbs surrounding Charleston, Mount Pleasant was originally a plantation owned by some amoral plutocrat named Jacob Mott and was the setting for what I am sure is a whole series of historic horrors that we just don't remember or at least try not to talk about anymore. But it's a part of us just the same.

The other thing a lot of people don't know about Mount Pleasant is that it got its name from an eighteenth-century eu-phemism for a vagina. That's right—*Mount Pleasant* is just co-lonial American slang for *vajayjay*. And after growing up here, I would say that's just about right. Mount Pleasant is a womb with an ocean view.

The year my mom died, there was a lot of change going on in my life as it was. Things had already started to get complicated, just on account of growing up. I was in the middle of my first year of high school at Wando, the largest high school in the whole state and seriously the worst place ever. There were four thousand students stretching across four grades, and it was obvious even to the most casual observer that there were just way too many of us wild Indians and not nearly enough chiefs. The teachers were as overwhelmed as we were. Everybody was just treading water, waiting for the rescue boats that never arrived.

I went to a Christian elementary and middle school, so I was supposed to just follow my friends on to the Christian high school, but I wanted to go to public school instead. I thought there would be more of a mix of kids. I was tired of the same old group of kids I'd been with since I was like, born practically. And to be honest, they were never all that nice to me. I didn't quite fit in. I thought maybe a change of scenery would help, but when you're a teenage girl, it's pretty much *Lord of the Flies* no matter where you wind up. Pure survival of the cutest. And much like my mom, I felt ill equipped.

My mom struggled with her self-image constantly. She was always looking in the mirror and making faces like she was disappointed every single time she saw herself. I used to think that was so sad and kinda stupid, because my mom was really beautiful; but now I notice myself doing the very same thing. I'm trying to make a conscious effort not to do that. I don't want a negative body image to be the part of my mom that lives on in me.

That summer before everything, I was excited, but I was nervous, too. I was starting a new school, and I had decided to work on finding some better friends. I was sick of kids who wanted to know who my parents were or where I lived or what my dad did for a living before they'd be friends with me. I didn't see why I had to use my parents' pedigree to compete socially as a teenager. And my parents didn't have a pedigree. So there was that. I was hoping Wando would be different, and it was. Wando was a come-as-you-are kid mill.

Hanging out with the A-list was never very important to me anyway, which makes me different from most everybody down here that I can think of. Charleston is very friendly on the surface, but before things get too far along, they'll want to know who your people are, how far back you go, what your stake to the land is, what private school your daddy graduated from, and how your granddaddy made his money. My daddy was from Texas by way of Huntsville, Alabama. So even though he was a navy pilot, in Charleston, where there is a naval air base on the outskirts of town, that wasn't exactly a golden ticket. My mom was South Carolina to the bone, but she was from Manning, which, as people say in Charleston, is not, well, Charleston.

I was born right here in Charleston. I had sprung up from good local soil, as they say. I had potential. But then I decided to go to a public school and said no to cotillion, which was like shooting my debutante dreams in the face. Nobody comes out in a white ball gown from Wando. My mom knew that, but she didn't care. She didn't make it personal. She let me make that decision for myself, which was so cool of her when I think about it now.

My decision made her different from a lot of her friends, although I didn't give it a second thought at the time. All the moms were probably sipping mimosas and chatting about their daughters' debut plans over bottomless brunches at the Obstinate Daughter, or in spring, at Poogan's Porch before it got too hot to sit out. My mom had to look at all those photos, and ooh and aah over how beautiful their daughters looked in their ball gowns, without being able to share any pictures of me wearing anything but cutoffs and a tee. I wonder if that hurt her feelings. If it did, she never let on.

I never had much social ambition. I never liked being the center of attention. I'm a renegade. And I suspect that under all the gracious Southern sweetness, my mom was a renegade, too. Oh, sure, she started out by marrying the sensible boy from her hometown and settled down behind a white picket fence and had two sons. But then I think she got bored. She had expected more from life. She longed for adventure. And that's when she met my dad. In the end, though, despite her robust inclinations, she turned out to be an ephemeral flower.

Whenever I see a group of paperwhites now, I think about my mom. People stay with you in little ways like that after they're gone. At first, I thought maybe my mom would come back and visit me as a ghost or a vision or in a dream. I was disappointed when she didn't materialize out of the mist like they do sometimes down here. I realize now that my mom is with me every time I blend a green shake, or fold a towel, or squeeze a lemon, or do any of the gazillion things she taught me how to do that you never think about until afterward.

I like paperwhites because they bloom in the spring before anything else pops up, and then later in the fall, when everything else is dying. A single paperwhite is supposedly bad luck, but together, they stand for hope and trust and faith and unconditional love. Positive virtues. Ephemerals never really die, they just go to sleep by the roots of tall trees and multiply underground. And then twice as many flowers come up the next spring. It's like they're immortal that way.

"There is nothing lonelier than a solitary paperwhite," my mom would say to me or herself or whoever happened to be standing close by, which I used to think was so embarrassing. "You see, Eva? They understand that they need one another if they're going to make a difference in this world. Remember that, sweetheart. Everybody needs their little cluster." I'd roll my eyes, because I knew where she was going. She was always telling me to make more friends, but I had plenty of friends; I just didn't like any of them.

At my mom's funeral, her casket was dripping in tasteful groups of amiable and peaceful paperwhites and white roses. Everything was white. Yet for some reason, in the pictures, there I am with a big bunch of sunflowers in my hand, like I'm Vincent van Gogh in fucking Arles or something. Those profuse midsummer field flowers and I really stuck out. Where did they even come from? I have no idea. That's just what happens to me. I'm always a little out of step, even though I really don't mean to be. I try to blend in. I want to be a paperwhite in a happy little cluster, but I'm not. I'm a sunflower. I make a statement all my own, whether I like it or not.

I don't remember a lot about my mom's funeral, to be honest. That whole thing is a blur. I remember I was wearing a black dress, obviously, which Beverly picked out for me at Sears. My dad had asked her to help me find an outfit. Going shopping for clothes with me was my mom's thing. I think it would have been too heartbreaking for him to stand in her place so soon. Not that he knew the first thing about how to shop for a teenage girl. I heard the sales associate ask Bev, "What's the occasion?" like I was going to my first formal or something. Inside, I was repeating, *Don't say it, please don't say it.* But I knew she was going to say it.

"Her mom's funeral," Bev whispered. The sales associate looked terrified, murmured something about condolences, and scurried off in the direction of women's dress shoes. That's how people are around me these days. They scatter like minnows when you're scooping your pail for chum.

I remember getting ready for the funeral. Bev was helping me zip up my dress, and I told her about the time I started crying when my mom said that one day I'd have boobs as big as hers. Beverly started laughing. "Eva," she said, "don't you know your mom got her boobs done in the nineties? You can't inherit fake boobs."

"Her boobs were fake?" I was completely startled and yet relieved at the same time. "Are you sure? Why wouldn't she tell me that?"

"Well, nobody likes to admit their boobs are fake, Eva. She

was probably just proud of them," Bev said, hooking my dress and handing me the nylons I had hidden under the covers, hoping she'd forget about them.

Learning this about my mom's boobs really freaked me out. I mean, this meant that my mom had kind of lied to me. A sin of omission at minimum. But I was so happy to know that I wouldn't wake up one morning and not be able to roll over. I didn't want big boobs. I'm a black belt in karate, and I love to surf. I like my center of balance right where it is, thank you very much. But I do wonder why my mom said that to me about my boobs. Did she think that would make me happy? Was that what she wanted for me? Would she have ever told me the truth? I have a lot of questions I'll never know the answers to, and that's one of the weird things about death. You're left with question marks, and you just have to live with them.

My brother Ben drove Bev and my brother John and me to the funeral. My dad drove with my uncle and cousins who had flown in from Texas. We listened to Blink-182 the whole way to the cemetery. I realize that alt-surfer punk rock is an odd choice when you're driving to your mom's final moments aboveground. But they had been my favorite band since my brother John introduced me to them the summer before. That song "All the Small Things" made me think about the way my mom noticed all the tiny details of her world. She would take pictures of everything and show them to my dad, one by one. The flower that opened on the side of the road, the bird that had stopped by on our windowsill, me in a dumb hat. There must have been millions of them.

My dad would look at every picture and smile at the beauty that he saw through her eyes, and they'd laugh and sigh and tell each other how cute I was even though I am 100 percent certain I looked like a total dork. My dad never got bored with those endless snaps. God knows I did. My mom told me she felt like the only person in the world when she was with my dad. He was like that. That was one of his superpowers. My dad was like the sun shining on your face.

The service was graveside in a small town called Florence, close to where my mom grew up in Manning. Just before the turn into the graveyard, we passed a beat-up old farmhouse with a sprawling family of rednecks out front. "Some people will sit on their porch all day long until somebody starts shooting," Ben said. I swear when we were leaving the funeral, I saw a person dead on that porch with the others just standing around the body, looking at one another, scratching their heads. I think they call that *dramatic foreshadowing*.

By the time we rolled up on the cemetery, there were already a few people there, standing around, looking shell-shocked. I saw the Wilsons there. Even Henry had come and had put on a suit, which looked weird. He usually looked like a skater rat. I had never seen him dressed up like a grown man before. He looked as uncomfortable as I felt. My dad's side of the family had all flown in from Texas, and my mom's people drove down from Manning, which was about an hour and a half north of Charleston. They all looked well turned out, but exhausted, and a little confused.

Everybody just stood at the grave for a while, stunned. Like nobody could believe what had happened. The autopsy revealed that my mom had died of a heart attack from a congenital heart defect that none of us had known she had. Even though the medical examiner had made it official, nobody could believe it. My mom was so vibrant. She practically glowed with life. Everybody just stood around for a while staring at that casket, and then looked over at me. I could tell what they were thinking. If I had been a problem before, now my daddy was really going to have his hands full. I was thinking that this was the first time my mom had ever shown up to anything early.

I remember tugging at those torturous sheer nylons during the sermon. I hated pantyhose generally, and today in particular, but Beverly had made me pull them on. It was one of the rare days in December when it was actually cold, and she worried about me getting chilly during the graveside service. I was grateful to her for worrying about me like that, so I wore the damn things. But now I hated how shiny they were in the sunshine as they suffocated every one of my pores. Just looking at them made me itch.

Before the reception line formed, my brother Ben, who I should mention was a Green Beret who had already done two tours in Afghanistan, looked at me meaningfully. It was the look he always gave me when he was about to issue marching orders and wanted me to pay very close attention, because he already knew I'd mess it up. He handled me like I was a loaded gun that might go off accidentally and shoot the translator.

"Eva, there are going to be a lot of people who won't look familiar to you, and they're going to want to pay their respects.

You're going to hear a lot of *I'm so sorry*s today, so just come up with a polite response, keep it short, and use the same answer all day long. That way you don't have to think about it or worry about saying the wrong thing," Ben said sensibly.

"And make sure to say thank you to everyone before you move on to the next person," said my brother John, who was as different from Ben as chalk is from cheese. Yet somehow, they made a kind of cute pair of mix-and-match separates. I was the odd sibling out. The baby half sister. The second-marriage sunflower.

I remember being jealous that my brothers had known our mom a lot longer than I had. They knew her before I was born, before she met my dad, before the heart condition that killed her made its silent entrance into her life. They knew her when she was young, as young as I am now, only way more chill because her mother didn't die when she was fourteen, when she still needed her.

I sat in the front row, looking at anything but my mom's casket. When Ben got up to speak, I choked up and started bawling, which was mortifying, but I couldn't help it. I just couldn't stop, and I didn't even know why I was crying. I mean, I did obviously know why, but I didn't feel the sadness yet in a way I could identify or name. It was happening involuntarily— all the waterworks went on, the snot and salt dripping everywhere, and yet I felt nothing. Still, I was unable to spit out a single sentence to anybody who was kind to me. Five women tried to hand me Kleenex. I took them all without even looking up or saying a single thank-you. My brothers watched me and just shook their heads. I suck at small talk, and that's a terrible failing in the South.

My dad gave the eulogy, and while I can't remember a word of what he said, I do know that was the first time I had ever seen him cry. That made me start bawling all over again. There was just something about seeing my dad, a strong, silent soldier, breaking down in front of everyone and being so vulnerable.

Afterward, we had a gathering at some place I'd never heard of, in a town I'd never been to before. It took like half a century to get there, over bumpy country lanes, and I had to pee so bad that by the time we got to the restaurant, I felt decades older. It's exhausting spending all day long in a pair of pantyhose in the sun, trying not to face reality.

CHAPTER 4

FROZEN BLUEBERRIES

It feels weird to say, but that summer after my mom died was one of the happiest times of my life so far. I mean, obviously, I missed my mom. So much. I can't even put it into words. My dad was right. It was hard, and long, and terrible to even begin to come to terms with what it meant that my mom was gone forever. And yet grief has its gifts to offer you, even though they can be difficult to unwrap.

There is something liberating about life once you've crossed the fall line and let yourself sink into a deep-sea depression, far beneath the swells, where the salinity is five times greater than the surrounding water, and everything floats. Nobody expects you to do anything. All the rules and responsibilities of normal life are suspended. It's almost like you died, too. Like you're a ghost of the fog, and the fog is a ghost of the sea. It felt peaceful being a ghost within a ghost.

In those first months after my mom died, it was just my dad and me sitting cross-legged on the bottom of the ocean in our own private brine pool. Come too close, and you will die from the salt of our tears. I know y'all are thinking, *But wait, Eva, you can't breathe when you're underwater*, but when you're a ghost, you can hold your breath for literal centuries. By the time you finally start to breathe again, you realize you've grown gills. You have adapted. You realize that you don't ever have to return to the surface again unless you want to. At that point, even breathing becomes optional.

My dad was traveling less that summer. He had been flying all over raising financing for a start-up tech company. He told his board he needed to stick closer to home so he could spend more time with me. Everybody at his work was so nice about everything and told him to take whatever time he needed. But truth was, my dad was jumpy—I could feel it, like an undertow. We took it super easy and spent good and important time together, though. Time I'll always be grateful for. We even went to California, and I saw the Pacific Ocean for the very first time. We found a little place by the water and ate West Coast oysters and watched a pod of humpback whales breach while the saffron sun dipped behind the purple hills of Catalina Island.

My dad really stepped up in those nine months. He was still my same dad, but I could tell that he was trying to be a mom to me also. He let me talk to him about the stupid stuff you overthink to death when you're fifteen. Idiot boys who had ghosted me, mean girls who were, well, mean to me. He got so excited when I got my black belt and even when my very first Instagram account started to build a following. He listened to it all without ever getting impatient. It was just like when he'd look at my mom's gazillion boring pictures of flowers and birds by the roadside. He paid attention to every dumb detail of my traumatized teenage life. That's how much he loved me.

I am so thankful that I got to know my dad a little better that year. I'm so glad that I got to see who he was as a person, and not just my dad, before he died. I think I saw a little bit of what my mom must have seen in him when she married him. My dad was a military guy, he kept his shoulders back, but he was also creative, and funny, and sweet, and a little bit of a dreamer. He had boundless, bouncy energy, kind of like a golden retriever. He could picture something, and then just by his telling you about it, you could see it, too, almost as if it were real. And you'd want to be a part of that story. My dad helped me imagine the possibilities in life. He helped a lot of folks do that.

In a way, in those days, my dad and I were like war buddies. We had been through something difficult together, something that nobody but us could understand, and that had bonded us differently from just a regular father and a daughter. That's one gift you get from a terrible loss. You develop an appreciation for what remains—just me, my dad, and Sully. We were the fragile and improbable life inside the bleached coral.

My sister-in-law Beverly had moved in with us right after my mom passed. It kind of happened without us really having to talk about it beforehand. It just seemed to make sense. My brother was deployed for a third tour in Afghanistan, she was missing her Ben, and all of us were missing my mom, so we just naturally gravitated toward one another, like seaweed that attached to the rocks. The three of us grabbed on to one another, anchored by grief, necessity, and freak circumstance.

Beverly kept the house going better than my mom ever did, to be honest. Bev is very organized. She's good at systems. Bev became the caring and loving woman at the center of our galaxy, who kept all our planets orbiting around her sun. This is just the kind of person you want around after a Big Bang. It was Bev who taught me how to stitch a hem, how to lock down your trash cans so the raccoons don't tear into them, how to unclog a kitchen sink or restart the furnace when the pilot light goes out. All important stuff I did not know. When my mom was alive, things could be a little chaotic. My mom went in a lot of directions at once, and we all loved that about her. She was invested, and she wanted to do it all. Only she couldn't.

We used to laugh and roll our eyes when my mom would come running in from Bible study five minutes late, grab her yoga mat, and go rushing off to Miss Melanie's, only to stop dead in the middle of the road and come running back inside to search for something she'd forgotten, making herself even later than before. Nobody minded my mom being a little scatterbrained or less than punctual. We always said it was because her heart wrote checks her time couldn't cash. That turned out to be prophetic.

So now Bev was there to teach me how to do my laundry, how to wash the gunk out of the air conditioner filter, how to bleach the grout, get wine stains out of white shirts, balance the books, pay the bills, or bake a birthday cake. Okay, I'm still working on the birthday cake, but I'm getting pretty good at sourdough cookies. The list of adulting skills I have Bev to thank for is long. Bev made it all so much less awful than it could have been, and I'm so grateful for her.

My dad didn't come to the table every night for family dinner like he used to when my mom was alive, but he tried to be positive and stay involved as much as he could. I could see that he was sad, but he didn't talk to me about it much. He tried to stay optimistic, at least around me, which may have been part of the problem. He never really gave himself time to grieve. I think he had it in his mind that he had to be strong for me, and I don't know, maybe he did.

So, Bev, my dad, and I held on tight, and life went forward, in the way that it does, because you have to live on, no matter how many skies have fallen. When my dad traveled, sometimes I'd stay at my friend Sadie's house, upping my surf game. My friend Sadie lived right on the water, so she was a legit surf rat, and she could shred a wave like nobody I ever saw before in real life, and that includes the boys. She surfed like she was born on a sled. I wanted to be just like her.

What Bev taught me about the household, Sadie taught me about the ocean. She taught me how to develop a good relationship with the sea, how to read the water, which is way more complicated than you might think. Sadie showed me how to tell which direction a wave's going to break by comparing the angle of the drift with the horizon line. She taught me how to find the top of a swell, when to surrender the crest, and how to fall off a wave without dying. All critical skills when it's just you, and the board, and the great gray-green mother.

After long days at the beach, soaring on sunlight and Starbucks, Sadie and I would watch movies in her rec room and stay up all night talking about basically everything and also nothing at all. Nobody ever yelled at us to go to sleep. We were down in the basement where no one could hear us. We may as well have been on the bottom of the ocean.

That house was like a summer beach cabana all year round. Nobody got up in your grille about anything. I loved sleeping over at Sadie's house. Her mom would bring us down bowls and bowls full of frozen fruit, and my favorite was the blueberries. Those icy blue balls were the most delicious thing I'd ever tasted, and we ate them by the fistful all summer long. It was a bad year for my family, but a really great year for blueberries.

My dad bought me my first car that summer. I had finally, after what felt like an entire century, managed to turn fifteen and apply for my permit. I had stayed at my friend Taylor's house that night before my birthday because my dad was out of town. She and her parents were obviously in on the big reveal. When my dad pulled up the next morning, they were like, "Eva, there's a surprise for you out front," and I was like, *Oh, great. What now?*

That's the thing about trauma. It will ruin surprises for you for the rest of your life. I hate surprises now, and this is a loss because I used to love them more than anything. But once you walk home after school one day and surprise! Your mom's dead! You're like, *Yeah, okay, let's just stick with the boring and predictable. I'm all stocked up on surprises.* So, when Taylor's mom said the s-word, I started searching for an exit.

Taylor said, "No, Eva, this is a good surprise. Come outside. Come on, you have to come and see." I looked up into Taylor's lawn-green eyes, pleading and sparkling with bottled-up effervescence. I could see from across the room that her mom was starting to tear up, and all because they were happy for me. I just couldn't disappoint them. So, I sucked it up and went outside, and that's when I saw my dad hopping out of his truck all giddy and bouncy like he used to get when he had some trick up his sleeve. He came galloping toward me, his hair all floppy and shining in the sunshine. When I saw the Jeep on the tow, I didn't know what to say. I was momentarily speechless.

My dad got to the porch, and grabbed me and hugged me really tight, and kissed me on both cheeks and then even once on the forehead, and tousled my hair. I was feasting on feels. Then he handed me the keys to my first truck, a white Jeep Wrangler, which looked like true love on four fat mud hogs. It was the first pure joy I had felt since I lost my mom. I tried not to feel guilty about it.

"I'm so proud of you, Eva. The way you've handled everything," he said, his voice sprinkled with emotion. His bright blue eyes twinkled with love and pride. "Losing your mom so young and still managing to grow up into such a beautiful, bright, and responsible young woman. If your mom were here, she'd be so proud of you, honey." I saw a tear slide down his cheek, then I turned and saw Taylor and her mom tear up. Would everybody just get a hold of themselves? Oh my God.

I started to laugh, and then I cried, too, imagining my mom, raining on us all with her embarrassing tears, while she apologized for making a scene because she loved us so much.

Then, for that one birthday afternoon, all the grief and shock of the last nine months just fell away. I started jumping up and down, like a normal teenager is supposed to do when her dad gives her her very first suffragette-white set of wheels. There's a whole thing about white cars in my family. I don't know what that's about, but I had become a part of the generational chain nonetheless. My mom's first car was a white Mustang convertible, and every one of her cars after that had followed in the same palette. Come what may, my mom always drove a white car. My brother John's first truck was white, too. Now I had my first white Jeep. It would have slayed my mom to watch me climb behind the wheel of my first white crawler. See what I mean about surprises? They're the worst, even when they're wonderful.

I felt really blessed to have a dad who was sweet enough to do this for me, who recognized how hard I was trying to be a daughter both he and my mom could be proud of. My dad understood that you never forget your first roller, and he sure AF did not skimp. He didn't go around scouting the used car lots for some rattletrap I could drive around in until I was old enough to be trusted with the real deal. This whip was pure Gucci. I immediately wanted to pimp that baby out with every accessory on the planet. I wanted my truck to look like a legit Chucktown crawler. But first, my dad and Beverly had to teach me how to drive.

Summer oozed and drawled through the hourglass like clumpy wet sand, while I tooled around in my fire new ride in search of myself. Then the first gusts of fall blew in. An evil damp rose up out of the ooze of the Florida Gulf Coast, and everything went to shit in the blink of an eye.

Surprise!

CHAPTER 5

I KNOW WHY THE REDFISH ARE SMILING

As fall scuttles in like a blue crab over the Low Country, the wind gets brisk and savory. You can see all the life of the marsh start to shiver. The cattails burst and disperse, the seed heads on the marsh get picked clean by the ravenous herons bulking up for the winter, and the cordgrass fades from lush green to a drab brown. The egrets settle onto their nests, oysters go on holiday, and the fishermen head out to sea, following the Carolina redfish into the intracoastal waterways. The redfish are easier to spot this time of year because they are forced to make their way out of the shallow marshes and into deeper water if they want to survive the winter.

Like a lot of us folks in the Low Country, redfish are cagey and quick. And this is especially curious considering their size. Redfish can be real heifers, given enough time to grow up. I think the biggest redfish anybody ever caught in South Carolina was seventy-five pounds and was over thirty-five years old.

The biggest guy I ever caught was only about twenty pounds, but still, he put up one hell of a fight. The boys had to help me haul that beast into the boat with a marlin net. Then we just threw him back.

I don't mind the sport of fishing, but I don't like killing anything. I'll bet the fisherman who caught that seventy-five-pound redfish, a fish that probably got bigger with every telling, made a lot of social bank on that salty yarn. He probably got invited to every oyster roast in the county that season. Monster redfish are the stuff that tall fish tales are made of down here. They are the hooch in the sweet tea of the Southern oral tradition.

I say that redfish are cagey because they are deceptive. They're born pretenders—lies built right into their DNA. There's a spot on their tail that looks just like an eye, and a stripe underneath that looks like a smile, so they trick predators into attacking the wrong end of their business, which gives them time to make their escape. Timing is everything in a carnivorous marsh. That's a pretty clever play for a fish, if you ask me. So the next time you think you see a redfish smiling at you, y'all remember, he's actually shooting you the moon.

My dad picked me up after school on that freaky and fateful Friday in September of 2016 during my interminable fifteenth year on Planet Earth. I was swimming out into the deep waters of my sophomore year at Wando. I was thinking that Friday would be like every other Friday of my life in the nine months since my mom died. Only on this particular Friday, my dad didn't take the left turn toward home as usual. Instead, he turned right, toward the Ravenel Bridge.

"Why are we going into Charleston?" I asked, but my dad didn't answer me. I could see his sneaky smile making crinkle lines from behind his aviators. He was up to something. Something that was beginning to feel suspiciously like a surprise.

"Change of plans," he said. "I have a little errand to run. You don't mind, do you, sweetie? You in a rush to be somewhere?"

"Well, I have a ton of homework to do," I said, and by this I meant I had a date to go wakeboarding with Blake. I wanted to go home. I did not want to go into town. I had a not-so-good feeling starting to kick up in the pit of my stomach. I looked down and noticed I was white-knuckling my phone. My dad pulled down his aviators and peered at me over his rims.

"It's a surprise, Eva. Are you actually going to be mad at me over a surprise?" My dad sounded a little exasperated, even though he knew how I felt about sudden changes in plans, so he finally gave up and told me what he was up to. "I met a woman. Her name is Ashley. She's in town for a few days from Florida, and I want you to meet her." I didn't like the sound of this one bit.

"She worked for the Women for Trump campaign. I met her at a party at Ben Carson's house in Palm Beach." I'm not even lying, but the hair on the back of my neck stood up the moment I heard her name spoken for the first time. A ghost from my future, looking backward.

My dad had been working with Dr. Ben Carson on drafting his national security policy when Dr. Carson was a candidate for president. Once he wasn't a candidate anymore, he threw a lot of fundraisers at his home in Palm Beach for the Trump campaign and was hoping to be a part of the Trump administration. My dad was usually invited to these parties, but he rarely went, since tickets cost like eight gazillion dollars and it wasn't really his crowd. How many times have I mused that, if only he had never gone to that stupid party, my life might have turned out so differently?

"Ashley and I got to talking that night and realized we have a lot in common. Since then, we've gotten pretty close."

"In a week?" I asked, but my dad didn't even hit Pause on his sales pitch. He was already in way over his head. Inside of seven days. Like I always say, once water finds a crack in your foundation, it will rush in and drown you.

"She's a good Christian woman like your mom was. And beautiful, too. Long story short—too late—Ashley's in town, and I wanted you two to meet."

I looked at him then, very seriously. "So you two are dating?"

"Just good friends, honey. Nothing like that," my dad said, and was that a giggle? He was lying through his teeth, and we both knew it, but only one of us cared.

"So why do I have to meet her, then?" You cannot outfox a teenage girl. I don't know why parents even try. We're the most strategic creatures in the deep blue sea, and we will see you coming from leagues away. In this case, though, it wasn't that hard. My dad had gone full-on cringe.

"She'll be a good role model for you, Eva. She's smart, pretty, successful, she's into social media, and she loves the Lord. Want to see what she looks like?" He handed me his phone out of his pocket. I immediately noted the boobs, which were perfectly matching twin globes and so obviously fake. I also noted that her picture was on his lock screen.

"Her name is Ashley Byers," my dad told me, trying to watch the road and my reaction at the same time. I was serving him Magritte. Just a hat with an apple for a face, floating inexplicably in a surreal blue sky. A car hit the brakes in front of us. I swear we almost wound up in the guy's trunk.

"Dad! God! Watch where you're going." I was already a nervous wreck. I didn't need a head-on collision as the cherry on top of my anxiety sundae.

"Sorry, honey, I'm just excited for you guys to meet. Isn't she gorgeous? And she's a wonderful person. So kind and loving. Can't you see that in her eyes?" I looked down at the smiling girl with long brown hair and the perfect plastic boobs rising up out of an airbrushed swimming pool like some kind of Maybelline mermaid. She had dead eyes.

"You met this girl at Ben Carson's house?" I asked. Off in the distance, I watched a fleet of shrimp boats chuffing round the bend headed toward Shem Creek. I wanted to become the spray off their bowsprits. I wanted to evaporate.

"Yes, at Ben's. I told you, she works for the Trump campaign."

"As what? The T-shirt gun girl?"

"Well, among other things," my dad said, and I could tell

he was starting to get triggered. I knew I was being rude. I knew he wanted me to be all excited about his new girlie, but down in my saline pool on the bottom of the sea, I felt the low rumble of continental drift, and I knew something was wrong.

"But you were just there. You've known her a week? And now her picture is your wallpaper? Pretty thirsty, Dad. Aren't you the one who taught me about playing hard to get?" It did feel thirsty. And very out of character for a low-key Low Country fighter pilot like my dad. He decided to ignore me and carried on with his own conversation like I cared. "She's a ballerina and a visionary who is going to change the world. She'll be a good influence on you, Eva." My dad made a hard left into the Marriott's porte cochere, stopped up short, and there she was, my new role model, in a pair of Daisy Dukes and a baby tee stretched across the twins that read TEAMWORK MAKES THE DREAM WORK.

"Hi, Eva, I'm Ashley," Boobs said, and I had to admit, she was hot. Even though I had just stared at her picture for five blocks, when you see her in person, it's arresting. Even unsettling a little. She's beautiful, but you could tell something was off. She looked sharp. Like if you touched her, you might bleed.

"Your dad's told me so much about you," Ashley said, and the way she said it sounded like what she'd heard wasn't all that great, which I knew couldn't possibly be the case. My dad was crazy about me. Ashley leaned forward to give me a kiss on the cheek. She missed me completely and pecked the air, which was totally on purpose. I noticed as she leaned in that there was a Beretta in her bra. This is not a metaphor.

"You don't mind hopping in the back seat real quick, though, do you, sweetie? So I can sit in front next to your daddy?" When she said *daddy*, she looked at my dad and winked. I just about barfed in my purse.

My dad had promised me he was never going to get married again, and while I understood intellectually that the time would come when he'd start dating again, I mean, it hadn't even been a year yet. And did it have to be this girlie? Shouldn't he have talked to me first? Given me a little bit of a heads-up? Didn't he owe me that much?

We all tried to be normal, the three of us, all gnawing on our private pretzel thoughts on the way back to Mount Pleasant. We grabbed coffee at the Brown Fox, and then they dropped me off at home and went on their merry way, overly sweet and way too fizzy like a grape Fanta. I've never been so relieved to see my dad's truck disappear down Preservation Place. I was hoping that would be the end of Ashley Byers. But by Sunday afternoon, while I was upstairs in my room painting a seaside landscape with Bob Ross playing peacefully in the background, a black swan came crashing through my blue sky.

"Eva, come downstairs, please," my dad called up to me, sounding phony as fuck. "Ashley is here, and I'm calling a family meeting." I immediately raised my deflector shields and turned up my tunes. Nobody said anything to me about Ashley coming over. As far as I knew, she was already on a plane back to bumfuck Florida and settled back into the primordial ooze from whence she had emerged. Since when was this person family? And while my dad had his faults—I could write you a list—*fake* had never been one of them. "Eva, come on down here now, darlin'!" he yelled a little louder and even phonier the second time. Or maybe it was the third.

"Um, no, I'm not coming down there for a family meeting, because Ashley is not my family!" I yelled down the stairs at him. I mean, come on, y'all. Give me a minute to process. I understood that my dad was a single guy, and I wasn't born yesterday. I understand the appeal of a young hottie with perfectly spherical boobs, but I guess I always thought my dad was smarter than that. And of all the classy single ladies dying to date my dad in Charleston, why did he go down to Miami and pick out some twenty-four-year-old busted-down ballerina slash T-shirt gun girl? It was so ick. Honestly, beyond ick. No, I wasn't supporting this kind of toxic folly.

"The only time we would need to talk about your situationship with Ashley is when you're ready to propose." I wasn't trying to be obnoxious. I always tried my best to be polite and respectful, especially when it came to grown-ups and even more especially when it was my dad. But I wanted him to know that I wasn't here for this discussion right now. He had put all of us in a very uncomfortable position, Ashley included. At that point, I just wanted them both to go away and leave me alone. That didn't happen, of course. Instead, my dad appeared in my bedroom doorway, eyes darting back and forth, like he was searching the corners for the right words and coming up empty.

"What's wrong with you? Why are you acting like one of the idiot boys I hang out with?" I wanted to throw my iPencil at him.

"Good news, Eva!" he said, the flare of his fauxthusiasm falling on the floor of my room with a thud like the dud that it was. "Ashley and I got married."

"You did WHAT?" I nearly spit my peanut milk macchiato across the room. My dad was looking like he was a squirrel trying to get an acorn past me and bury it in the backyard before I caught on. I don't know why he would try something like this with me. I was always three steps ahead of him. We thought the same. We were spooky connected. But this cringe play with Ashley had really thrown me for a loop. Suddenly, I felt a panic rising up inside me.

"Well, Eva, now that your mom's gone, you need someone, a mother figure in your life." I watched my dad's eyes shimmer in the light of the glowing superlatives that I think he thought he meant. "Ashley can be that person in your life. Ashley was a ballerina."

"Swimsuit model slash ballerina. I know how to google."

"She's taught lots of young girls to dance and has experience helping girls your age."

"So I need help now? What happened to thank you for being such a responsible, well-adjusted young woman that my real mother, my actual and recently deceased mother, would be proud of?" My dad was looking at me, startled and just this side of pissed off. I took a couple of cleansing breaths and adjusted my tone. I didn't really want to fight. But this was just so out of the blue and off-brand for my even-keeled dad. He was calm and steady in choppy water. Now, he seemed like he was all froth and churn.

"I just know you're going to love her as much as I do, Eva. Just give her a chance. You'll see I'm right. After you've lived with her for a while, you'll feel differently."

"Wait, she's moving in?" That part hadn't landed until right that moment.

"Well, of course she's moving in, Eva. She's my wife now, and she's your stepmother." My dad was looking at me like I was the crazy one. "We're gonna be one big happy family. Just trust me, honey. Ashley is the best thing for both of us. She's a gift from the Lord. I think Renee sent her to us, so we wouldn't be so sad and miss her so badly."

I realized right then and there that the dad I thought I was talking to on Friday morning had already ceased to exist. That guy hadn't been there for at least a week, and I hadn't even noticed. Maybe he'd never even existed at all. "Where is Bev going to live now?" I asked suddenly. I could not imagine life without Beverly. I refused to lose Beverly. I couldn't wait to call her. She was not going to believe this.

"There's room enough in our house for all of us chickens," my dad said cheerfully and put his arm around my shoulder. Sure. Easy for him to be chipper. He had just fallen head over heels with the boob goddess from Bikiniland. "Nobody has to go anywhere. We'll all just figure it out and make it work together. Now what do you say? Family meeting?"

Of course I had to go downstairs and attend the fake family meeting, and I fake listened to the fake feelings they both were just dying to share. I didn't say what I really thought. I kept it together. I didn't spontaneously combust. I didn't burn down the house like I wanted to. I minded my manners. I said, "Congratulations," and all the boring courtesies you're supposed to say, even though nobody really cares if you mean it or not. I sat through that whole meeting and smiled like a redfish, and the first chance I got, I shot upstairs to my bedroom and FaceTimed Bev.

I was like, "Oh my God, Bev, my dad married some twenty-four-year-old ballerina Barbie he met like five minutes ago, and now she's moving in. What are we going to do?" These words exploded out of me like a giant shredder wave ripping toward shore. I was trying hard not to scream. I absolutely refused to let myself scream. And then of course, I did scream, only quietly, inside my head.

"What the fuck?" Bev said. "Wait, hold up, Eva. Did you just say your dad got married? Without telling you first? And to somebody you'd never met before?"

"Yes, yes, and YES!" I said, and noticed I was on the verge of hyperventilating. I looked around for a paper bag, just in case. "I met her for the first time Friday, and he said they were just friends. I mean, Bev, what the fuck?"

"Eva, breathe. And don't cuss. Fuck! What was he thinking? Are you still breathing? Okay, good, now slow down and tell me everything." Bev was trying to be very reasonable, but I could tell her head was ready to explode just like mine was.

"I don't know. She's hot, I guess, although I don't get the hype. I mean, she lisps like she's still a baby. News flash: You're an adult, talk like one."

"Is it on purpose?" Bev asked me to send her a picture of

Ashley. I sent her the first shot that came up on Google. It was of course the boobs-on-the-water shot my dad had on his phone. Bev looked at it, and her face went white, and then kinda greenish, and then ghost white again. "Go over to Sadie's," Bev said, sounding just like my brother Ben. "Go surfing. Eat frozen blueberries. Don't give this male midlife foolishness another thought. I'll talk to him. Don't worry. I'll call you when I get to the house."

That sounded like the best idea I'd heard all day. I grabbed Sully, jumped in my whip, briefly thought about the fact that I didn't have my license yet and technically needed another licensed adult in the car with me, and then gunned off anyway. Whatever. Rules were for girls with mothers who survived to see them graduate high school, and with fathers who made sense. I pulled out and drove over to Sadie's, praying that Johnny Law would look the other way just this once. I didn't want my permit to be suspended. Independent transport had just become situation critical.

When I got to the beach, I told Sadie what happened, and she hugged me and told me not to worry, that dads could do dumb things sometimes, but they usually came to their senses eventually. I felt better after she said that. Then we grabbed a big bag of frozen blueberries and sat on the sand while the tide ebbed, and googled the shit out of Ashley. I didn't find much about any ballet career or about teaching teenage girls. But we did find her swimsuit model portfolio under some fake name that sounded cheesy.

"She doesn't look very *Swan Lake* to me," Sadie said, kicking sand at a ghost crab closing in on us from the water's edge.

"More like one of those girlies on the calendars behind the counter at the Jiffy Lube, right next to the blue paper towel dispenser."

Then Sadie and I got the giggles and called everyone we knew and texted them Ashley's swimsuit-modeling page, and we all rolled our eyes. My girls all knew what they were looking at. My boys knew, too, but it landed differently. They were like, "Really sucks for you, but, dude, your stepmom is fire. When can we meet her?" Boys really are such idiots.

CHAPTER 6

SPLIT ENDS

How do you solve a problem like Ashley Byers? This is a question I have been turning over and over in my mind since that first day she pushed me into the back seat of my dad's Jeep, sucked down my childhood through a straw like it was a Diet Cherry Coke, and burped. From that parking lot forward, I became auxiliary to my dad's life. Ashley moved in, I got pushed aside, and Bev, my rock and the center of my motherless galaxy, moved out within a week.

Ashley was over-the-top nice to me in the beginning, but mostly just in front of my dad. I could tell that there were wheels within wheels within wheels inside her head spinning every time she lisped at me. Even when she wasn't saying anything, you could still see them whirring in the background. She had the fixed gaze of an apex predator. Intense. Hungry. It was hard to say what she was building up to. If you had told me then, I would have rolled my eyes and said, *Don't be ridiculous*. But I would have been wrong about that.

Ashley and I tried to do stuff, just us. We tried to get a vibe going. We had lunch downtown. We went shopping. It wasn't terrible. I mean, it's lunch and shopping in Charleston. I'm majorly privileged to be able to do stuff like that; I'm not even complaining. But would I have rather been shopping with my mom or my girlies? Of course. Was Ashley super thirsty and socially awkward? Oh my God, totally. Was I embarrassed when she told the people behind the counter in the fancy milled soap store down on King Street that we were sisters? I could have died right there on the spot. But I did my best to roll with the tide. I really wanted her to like me, but I could tell she did not like me at all, and it wasn't even personal. I was just in the way.

It's difficult to explain, but when I looked at Ashley, I could just tell something had come unglued somewhere important. I think most people felt it, right from the jump. She was striking—smoking hot, actually—but looking at her was like looking through a window. You could see right through her to the other side, like she was a vampire or something. You take a picture of her, but when you look at it later, nobody's there. It's only then that you realize you've been having lunch and going shopping and smelling milled soaps with the undead.

One day before it got too cold, Ashley and I planted succulents in mason jars and set them out on the porch while my dad looked on, giddy as a blue crab at sunset. The plants died because Ashley never watered them like she said she would, and then, naturally, she blamed their untimely demise all on me. One time, she tried to give me advice about a boy I liked, which

I did not take. I mean, okay, I was single, and I wanted a boy-friend pretty badly, and apparently I was terrible at romance. But I wasn't taking any tips from somebody who married some old fool she'd known for only thirteen days. Even if the old fool was my dad.

The honeymoon phase did not last more than a couple of weeks for our new happy family. Before Halloween even arrived, Ashley was serving wicked stepmom. She was bossing me around in a way that my actual mom never did. I didn't say anything. I'm not good at confrontation. I was a nice Charleston girl trying to keep the peace. No fighting words. Just lots of awkward silences followed by furious scribbling in my diary later. I adopted a policy of nonviolent resistance. In other words, I ignored the bitch, only to discover later that the worst thing you can do to a possible malignant narcissist is pay them no mind. That makes them go even crazier just so you'll notice them.

Eventually, everything became my fault. I didn't particu-larly care one way or the other what Ashley thought of me. But I loved my dad more than anybody else in the world, and she was coming between us on purpose. Ashley would blow up the little stuff I did wrong to get my dad pissed at me. She blamed all the problems in the house on me. Meanwhile, I wasn't the one sucking all the air out of the room. I have appropriate boundaries, unlike some people.

Still, no matter how it started, or how I felt about things, they were married now. That was a fact, and I'd better get used to it. I thought about what my mom would say. She'd tell me to be sweet and positive; to try my hardest to find a way to make the situation better for everybody involved. She'd say God doesn't make mistakes and then tell me some dumb story about a bird, or a flower, or a lonely frog who lost her lily pad but then found another one that was even better, so it was just a blessing in disguise all along. She'd tell me to be happy my dad found somebody, so he didn't have to be lonely.

I started that very day trying to make more positive choices. I did a full 180. I tried to give my dad the benefit of the doubt and be understanding. I cut Ashley slack, and trust me, she needed miles of rope. Did it work? I don't know, I guess for a little while. I'm pretty sure that it never really mattered much either way in the end. I needn't have troubled myself. I think with Ashley, you're either useful to her or you're useless in general and should probably just go ahead and disappear. I did not disappear. I became the sugar in Ashley's gas tank.

Meanwhile, my dad and Ashley were acting like a couple of love-pilled idiots, so PDA it was beyond disturbing. They were always together, did everything together, went everywhere together, and wherever they went, they were embarrassing. Ashley even went with my dad on business trips. I was happy about this, because I got the house to myself. But I could tell it was uncomfortable for my dad. Ashley never dressed appropriately for any situation. My dad's clients were four-star generals and CEOs. I could just imagine their faces when Ashley strolled into a top security meeting in her slut drag du jour and her MAGA cap. There aren't enough eye rolls in the world to survive that level of yuck.

Ashley's insatiable need for my dad's undivided attention drove a wedge between my dad and me, which was bad enough, but she also alienated him from everybody else in his life. My dad didn't see his friends anymore, and he had a lot of them. He had serious rizz. He had owned a restaurant in town at one point, and so everybody in town knew and liked him. When my mom died, everybody pitched in to help. All the neighbors and the church ladies brought food over for months and always checked in on us. Now, nobody stopped by.

It was obvious that my dad's friends didn't approve of Ashley, but they were trying to be patient and wait it out. I think we all hoped my dad would come to his senses and leave Ashley in the dust. Until then, though, people observed a careful perimeter. I couldn't blame them. As for me, well, I didn't have many choices. I was in high school. Where was I gonna go? So I spent a lot of time in the water. And I took up running. From the moment Ashley moved in, I was in perpetual motion. And waterlogged. I was always vigilant, just waiting for the monster to emerge. And then, one day right before Halloween, she did. I had just come in from the beach, and for some reason, she noticed my hair was frizzy and decided to do something about it, like immediately.

"You know what we do for dry, frizzy, and damaged hair like yours, Eva?" Ashley lisped coquettishly. She came right up to me the second I walked through the door, before I'd even taken off my shoes, and started running her fingers through my straw tangles. She made disapproving clucking sorts of sounds with her mouth and pouted and batted her eyes at my dad like, *See how maternal I can be? Even with this troubled and incorrigible brat of yours?* Now, I will admit, I do get a bad case of beach head after surfing all summer. I mean, she wasn't wrong. The sun and salt takes a toll on my normally lustrous and shimmering tresses. That's my story, and I'm sticking to it.

"What? It's fine, Ashley. I'll condition later," I said, and pulled away from her.

Ashley looked directly at me, her eyes hardening into two smoldering black coals. "No, we'll condition it NOW," she said with a level of commitment that didn't really match the situation. Were we still talking about split ends?

"I told you, I don't have time right now. I have to do my homework, fold my laundry, paint my ceiling, and commit second-degree larceny," I said, and trust me, I was talking about everything plus my homework.

"I said right now, young lady," Ashley said, so loud it even startled Sully. "*Later* is too late. NEVER put off until tomorrow what you can so easily do right this instant. Why are you always so difficult, Eva, when I'm only trying to help you?" Ashley set her chin and looked meaningfully at my dad, waiting for him to pick a lane. I waited, too, noticing that her lisp had miraculously disappeared. Bev was right. It was all on purpose.

Ashley and I just stood there for a moment, locked together in hate, waiting out the awkward shuffling back-and-forth of my father's loyalties. He looked up at us both, and I could see that he was wishing that the earth would open and suck him under. I wasn't worried, though. I was 100 percent sure my dad wouldn't throw me under the bus over split ends. We were best friends. Deep sea buddies. Hand in hand to the end.

"Eva," my dad said, staring down at his shoelaces, "let Ashley condition your hair right now, or I'll take away your car."

CHAPTER 7

MANIC PANIC

Whenever I walk down by the Battery in Charleston, I think about all of the gypsies, tramps, thieves, and vagabonds who have stumbled along the waterfront since the town began way back in 1670. Charleston always was and still is a beautiful trash heap. The city itself is built on top of an ancient landfill piled high with oyster shells—toss-aways from centuries of Native American oyster roasts built up to the point that they became a peninsula made of the remains of ancient picnics jutting out into the bay.

Eventually, picnic peninsula got big enough to form a harbor where ships sailed in from all over the world, carrying all manner of colonial-era Eurotrash into town. But of all the charlatans, drunkards, scallywags, and one-eyed jackals that have traipsed along the cobblestones of Rainbow Row, my favorites have always been the pirates.

When I was little, I wanted to be a pirate when I grew up. My dad told me that wasn't a good plan, since pirates were not good people, and besides, there was no such thing as lady pirates back then anyway. And even if there had been, they wouldn't have been allowed to own property, so why would I wish for a future like that? I would remind him that no lady could own property in Charleston at that time, sinner or saint. That's when he'd gently suggest that while that may very well be true, perhaps I'd like to choose a better icon, somebody more positive, like Madame Curie or Sally Ride. Maybe Meryl Streep.

My dad was right about Marie Curie and Sally Ride and even Meryl Streep—I love her and her daughters—but he was dead wrong about the lady pirates. In fact, there was a lady pirate who lived right here in Charleston, and her name was Anne Bonny. Anne was a tomboy like me, only she had flaming red hair and an independent streak a country mile wide. Nobody could tame Anne Bonny. Well, is it any wonder? She was so good with her sword that she stripped her fencing instructor naked in the town square . . . one button at a time.

Anne grew up in Mount Pleasant like I did, and also like I did, she got bored living out in the middle of nowhere with nothing to do. So she did what bored Mount Pleasant teenagers have done for centuries—she went into Charleston looking for trouble, and she found it. Anne started hanging out down by the Battery and fell in love with a dashing bad boy named Jim Bonny, and within weeks, they had eloped in secret. When Anne's father, a prominent lawyer in Charleston, found out, he pitched a colonial fit and disowned his daughter right on the spot. So the very next night, Anne burned her daddy's plantation house down to the studs.

After that, Anne and Jim sailed away to Barbados, where Anne ran into a new pirate who was taller and hotter than Jim and who wore these fashion-forward striped pants that earned him the nickname of Calico Jack. Next thing you know, Jim is out, Calico Jack is in, and a whole new chapter began for Anne on the high seas beyond Charleston Bay, sailing free and unafraid through the Devil's Triangle in the golden age of pirates.

I loved Anne Bonny because she didn't apologize for being who she was, and she wasn't pleasant or agreeable the way Southern ladies are supposed to be. She had a terrible temper, she could be a downright mean drunk, and she was known to steal other people's ships just for the lols. Nobody could figure out how she managed to survive into young adulthood with such a difficult disposition, but somehow, Anne managed to do just exactly as she pleased without getting murdered or burned at the stake or shunned or pilloried. Although the town did try to hang her twice.

Anne was a true progressive for her day. She had a gay best friend even though nobody was out or proud or anything like that in 1720. He was known as Pierre the Pansy Pirate, and he ran the local coffee shop/dress shop/hair-and-makeup salon down on Chalmers Street and made the ball gowns for every debutante in town. One night, a French merchant ship chugged into harbor. Anne and Pierre robbed that trading ship of every scrap of silk and velvet. Pierre made Anne a pair of couture black velvet knickers, which she wore Amazon-style. She could often be seen sailing out of Charleston Harbor on her ship the *William*, named after her father, standing bare-breasted on the prow, one hand on the hilt of her sword, the other holding a long silk scarf that danced in the wind behind her.

Sometimes, when I start to feel anxious, I imagine that I'm Anne Bonny, standing at the helm of my ship in velvet knickers like a terrifying figurehead, brave and intrepid. When I was little, I used to have these really messed-up dreams that my parents died in some really fucked-up way. Then I would see their gruesome corpses chasing me and begging me to help them. But there was nothing I could do. I couldn't help them. I would wake up hysterical and run down the hall. I'd climb in bed with my parents and lie in between them and squeeze my eyes shut while my mom rubbed my back until I fell back asleep.

My panic attacks start with this prickly feeling in my fingers, and then it moves into the top of my nose, and next, my whole face flushes pink. Then I get this metallic taste in my mouth, and my thoughts get obsessive and circular. I start to feel like I can't breathe, like I'm going to faint or die or throw up or poop in public, and just the thought of all that causes the next wave of panic to swell and crash. I literally get afraid of being afraid. It's a vicious cycle.

The first time, my mom said it was probably just another bad dream or maybe night terrors. She'd tell me to think of pleasant things, imagine that I was in my favorite place in the world. I'd imagine I was on the deck of my pirate ship, sailing bare-breasted to Barbados, just like Anne Bonny. And it helped, until the sun rose, and I had to get on that school bus.

For a while, the panic attacks subsided, but then without any warning at all, right around the time I started middle school, they picked back up again. I only noticed because my mom pointed out that I had started biting my nails and picking at my cuticles so badly that they were bleeding.

"Why are you doing that to your fingernails, Eva?" my mom asked like she was disappointed in me.

"I don't know," I said. "I just started doing it. I don't know why."

"Well, stop it. That's a VERY bad habit," my mom scolded, taking my hands into hers and examining my bloody stumps. "This looks terrible. How are you going to get a manicure now, young lady? Don't you want to have pretty nails?" She asked me these questions like biting my nails was a decision that I ought to have weighed more carefully in advance. Like I should have realized that if I was going to opt for wrecking my cuticles, I should just give up on polite society altogether. I was biting my nails out of anxiety. It wasn't a choice. I couldn't help myself. Still, my mom was right. My fingernails were a hot mess.

After the nail incident, I started getting anxiety attacks on the school bus again. This was a major setback. I'd get sick to my stomach and throw up in my seat, which is about the most embarrassing thing that you can do on a school bus in front of all your friends. Why was this happening to me? Was it the movement of the bus? Was it gravity? Was it terminal cancer? My folks thought maybe it was my vision, so I went to the optometrist, and nope. It wasn't my eyes. It was my old frenemy panic, come back for an unannounced visit. Then, of course, my mom died, and my panic went next level.

There was this one time at school, I was really busy—I had

a lot going on that day. A zillion things were going through my head at the same time. I hit critical mass or something and suddenly started asking myself stupid first-world questions like *Why am I here? Why am I doing all of this? Why am I trying so hard when it's all so pointless? Why am I thinking these things? Why am I asking myself these ridiculous questions?* I don't know why I thought these things, but I did. In fact, I couldn't stop thinking them, and it totally freaked me out. I sat down at my desk, put my head down, and basically blacked out. When I came to, I asked to be excused, and I called my dad.

I was trying to sound casual, but truth be told, I was pretty freaked out.

"Hey, Dad. Howzit going? I'm fine, but I don't know— something just sort of happened. I was just sitting at my desk, minding my own business, when I got really dizzy and really nauseous, and then I fainted a little bit on my desk."

"Did you have your coffee this morning?" he asked me. "You might not have enough caffeine in your system." While this seemed like an odd and very un-dad-like response to your daughter telling you she just fainted in class, in my dad's defense, I was a pretty religious coffee drinker even then. My dad had let me start drinking coffee when I was still young enough for it to stunt my growth. Which explains a lot. So my dad wasn't totally off base. I guess he thought I had gone into caffeine withdrawal or something. "It's just the midday slumps," he told me. "Either your blood sugar dropped or you need a little caffeine is all. Go get a sweet coffee after school. Two birds, one stone. You'll be fine. See you at dinner."

So I did what he said. I went to the Brown Fox after school and grabbed an enormous sweet macchiato with two extra shots. And I did feel better. Maybe my dad was right. But then a couple of weeks later, same thing. Only this time, the coffee cure didn't take. I googled my symptoms, and sure enough, there they all were in a bulleted list, right there in blue and white. I had an anxiety disorder. Classic case. So the next time I felt panicky, I called my dad and laid it out for him. "I'm having another panic attack at school," I told him. "It's not caffeine withdrawal, though, Dad. I have an anxiety disorder."

"Nah," my dad said. "You're too young to have anxiety or a disorder. Are you sure you had enough coffee today?"

I don't know why my parents had such a hard time recognizing that I had an anxiety disorder. They both had the very same problems with panic. My mom was anxious about all kinds of stuff that she made up in her head—the way she looked, how skinny or fat she was, what she ate for lunch, going to the doctor, whether she looked as good as Melanie across the street, what God thought about her, what my dad thought about her, bills that were not getting paid on time. Spiders. Her own mom and dad. She had a long list.

My dad had PTSD from the war, but he went to counseling for that before I was born and fixed it, although I could tell it crept up on him sometimes late at night. So they both knew about anxiety. They knew plenty. But I think that maybe they just couldn't face that a child raised in the golden dawn of their bright romantic future could be touched by the dark panic in their pasts.

After Ashley moved in and the cold war began on Preservation Place, I started having some pretty dark thoughts again. Maybe it was hitting me on a different level that my mom was gone forever and that Ashley was there to stay. Plus, I felt really disconnected from my dad, who was my port in every storm. I started thinking stuff like *My mom's gone, my dad doesn't care about me, no one will even care if I disappear, so what am I even sticking around for anyway?*

I knew enough to recognize when my thinking was turning dangerously toxic, and I needed to say something to somebody who could help. So one night, when the noise in my head got loud, I went downstairs to my dad and Ashley's room. I never did this before. I'd stayed out of that room since she moved in. God knows what I'd find in there. I didn't want to find out. But I needed to tell my dad I was in trouble.

"Listen, I'm sorry to bother you guys, but I'm having a major panic attack," I said, and then I just stood there appearing apparitional and odd, like I was made of ectoplasm. My dad and Ashley both sat straight up in bed in tandem, staring at me like *Sweet jumping Jesus, what do we do with her now?*

"I'm scared of myself, Dad," I said, shattering the fourth wall. My dad snapped out of it, leaped out of bed, put his arm around me, brought me into the living room, and sat me down on the couch. He put a blanket around my shoulders because I was shaking all over. I felt like I couldn't breathe. Ashley followed behind, topless and annoyed. My dad just sat there freaking out right along with me. Ashley looked disgusted with us both.

My dad finally got up and called Pastor Dan, even though it was like almost midnight. That's what my dad did when he was out of answers. He looked to God, which more often than not meant calling Pastor Dan, who was usually the closest thing to the divine that we could reach on the spur of the moment. I felt so grateful that Pastor Dan came out that late at night just for me. Unfortunately, he really didn't know what to do for me either. So we all just prayed, and I think everybody felt better, except Ashley, who was way over my momma drama. When the preacher left, Ashley went into the bedroom and came out shaking a bottle of pills. "Here, Eva, take one of my Valiums," she said. My dad looked like he was going to intervene, but didn't.

"No, thanks, I'm okay now. I don't like to take those kinds of pills," I said, which was 100 percent true. I did not say this to be mean. My mom had taken Xanax for a while when she was having trouble sleeping (see former list of things my mom worried about), and she didn't realize you couldn't mix those pills with wine. Ashley looked pretty butt hurt, shrugged, pirouetted, went back into the room, and slammed the door.

The next day, when I got home from school, I discovered that the memory board I had on my wall where I had put all my favorite pictures of my mom was gone. It had been replaced with a new board, with pictures of my dad and me. Ashley had completely disappeared my mother. All of the pictures of my mom, and I mean every single one, had been wiped from my room. I have no idea what she did with those pictures. I never did get them back. They were locked away somewhere in a sunken chest, at the bottom of the sea. Ashley had a special genius for retribution.

I think one of the reasons people are fascinated with pirates is because pirates are always in search of something they've lost and are willing to risk anything to find it. They'll spend their energy until their dying breath in some doomed pursuit of whatever this thing is that they've lost and are trying desperately to recover. Like the boy on *Outer Banks* who's always searching for his dad, who was lost at sea. Or like my dad, searching for my mom inside his marriage to Ashley. I think we're all a little like pirates when it comes to things we've lost. We're all engaged in a search and recovery mission for some treasure that's already gone, or maybe never existed at all.

That's another reason I like Anne Bonny. Instead of hunting for somebody else's lost riches, she was searching for the gold of her own rich history. Even though legend holds that Anne eventually reformed and became a respectable lady, I am skeptical. I'll bet that when nobody was looking, Anne was back out there on the water, probably floating on a board like I do now, alone in the arms of the gray-green mother, searching for the treasure she'd left behind. I like to think that she found it.

CHAPTER 8

NO, EVA, THERE IS NO SANTA CLAUS

My mom died in December, a few weeks before Christmas, so we just forgot about Christmas altogether that year. I think my dad and I went to the movies. So the first Christmas with Ashley was also the first time we had celebrated it since we lost my mom. My dad was full of the holiday spirit, humming carols and decking the halls. Well, he was in love. I was not. And the whole thing made me a little nauseous. I was excited about driving into the woods and finding our tree and having the whole house smell like Fraser fir, the way it used to, when my mom was alive. This is when Ashley decided to announce that she was allergic to real Christmas trees, and so we had to get an artificial one.

I don't know why, but of all the scandalous, fucked-up shenanigans that Ashley had pulled in the four long months since she rolled into town and blew up my life, this one stands out as singular and cruel, not to mention wholesale tacky. Was she

actually imagining that we, the Benefields, yearly finders, cut-
ters, and keepers of the nine-foot fir, would put up an artificial
tree? Not on your life, sweetheart.

Since my very first Christmas, or at least as many as I could
remember, we'd all hop in the family raft and head up to North
Carolina, where my dad would cut down the biggest tree in the
forest like he was Clark Griswold, drag it out of the forest, and
throw it into the back of the truck. We'd haul it back to Mount
Pleasant, singing carols all the way back over the river and
through the woods home. I'm not even kidding. We were the
most normal, hap-hap-happiest goddamn family since Santa
first slid his fat ass down the chimney. My dad would bake his
famous sourdough cookies, and the whole house would smell
like sugar and vanilla and pine. We'd put out cookies and milk
for Santa every Christmas Eve, although I caught on pretty
early that Santa wasn't the one eating them. Sully always looked
super guilty when my mom picked up the empty cookie plate
on Christmas morning.

When Ashley declared that she was hyper allergic to ever-
green and could even go into spontaneous anaphylactic shock
if she even so much as got near a conifer, I looked at my dad
and rolled my eyes. I was like, *Oh, man, are you actually gonna
let this go down like this on Christmas? Are you going to endorse a
fake tree in our front room?*

My dad hesitated. I know he knew this was a critical moment. I saw him see what this meant to me. "Okay, family," he
said, rubbing his hands together, trying to generate a holiday
warmth that did not exist. "Let's hop in the truck and head on

over to Home Depot and pick out the Benefield family Christ-mas tree." And that's where we found it. At Home Depot. In the seasonal aisle, underneath the cases of Duraflame logs and the bags of fat wood. I hung out in the art supply aisle. I refused to participate in the tree selection, even though my dad gestured to me three times to come over and help pick one out. I was like, *I just—I can't.* I bought a blank journal and a calligraphy pen. Ashley and my dad checked out with their basic-bitch plastic tree that I refuse to think or write about ever again, the end.

After the massacre of that family Christmas tradition, Ashley stormed the rest of my mom's cute little house. I was familiar with dark Barbie's taste in home decoration by then, so I was bracing for an assault. I looked at my dad, willing him to make eye contact with me so he could see the sheer terror in my soul and do something. Instead, he patted me on the head like I was Cindy Lou Who and said we should be happy that Ashley was finally settling in and making our place feel more like home. The Grinch had stolen his dad instincts and his design sense.

Within a week, our little house with the good bones on Preservation Place wasn't my mom's cozy, cute home anymore, which was sad, because my mom was a talented homemaker. Ashley wiped my mom from that house like the grease from last week's fish fry. She took my mom's pictures off the walls and rearranged all the furniture. The mirror over the fireplace with the little inlaid white birch daffodils that my parents bought on their honeymoon in North Carolina, the pictures of my mom and the boys at their weddings and graduations, my mom and me in front of our fresh, authentic, not plastic or pink Christmas tree, wearing Santa hats when I was eight.

My mom and dad and me when I got my black belt, in the silver frame he got in a shop on Pennsylvania Avenue in DC. All the little touches my mom had fussed over and shopped for and carried home and artfully arranged went out with the recycling. Ashley disappeared it all, except for one painting of golden pears that my neighbor rescued from the curb and gave back to me last year. It's now hanging above my couch.

Next, Ashley painted just about the whole house (not my room, thank you very much) in varying shades of black. I'm not even kidding. It could not have been an accident. It was intentionally evil. I'm talking the front door, the back door, the baseboards, the mantel, the floors, the cupboards. Everything. Everywhere. Black. They even installed black onyx countertops in our kitchen. I mean, who paints the inside of a house in the woods black? And at Christmas? It's twisted.

You have to understand. I'm an artist. I take pigment personally. I almost physically itch when colors collide. And I like color. I'm a fan. Black is the literal opposite of color. It's the entity that annihilates all hues. This crime she had committed against my mom's beautiful, naturally lit, soft taupe and petal-pink house really blew up my brain. Our house was already dark. The idea was to bounce light, not suck it up into a black hole of hideousness. "Calm down, Eva. Don't get so upset. It'll all come together in the end, you'll see. Have a little faith in Ashley," my dad said. But she never even managed to get the doors put back on the kitchen cabinets. We finally fixed every-thing before short selling the house after my dad's death.

I'm sorry, but I don't care how much gentle Jesus you have in you, it's damn near impossible to be Christlike when you're living under the same roof with that level of aesthetic aggres-sion. Ashley tore the place up for no reason, committing act after act of color cruelty, and felt persecuted if we objected to any of it. She held us hostage with her fake martyrdom. That's when I learned that there are folks in this world who walk around feeling like victims, who aren't victims at all. They are the worst kinds of bullies.

This was around the time I started getting close with my friend Roxy, who was on my lacrosse team, and also in my third-period art class. Art was my favorite subject. Roxy was only there to check a box on her way to becoming a famous photographer. Everybody loved Roxy. She's one of those girls who everybody thinks is cool because you can tell she gives exactly zero fucks about, well, anything really. Roxy had this reddish-gold hair and apple cheeks; she looked like an ironic Strawberry Shortcake. Roxy thought everything was funny, es-pecially the dark stuff. I was like, *Come over to my house, girlie. You'll die laughing.*

I got the feeling that Roxy was sad about something, but she didn't ever talk about it, and I didn't ask. None of us did. Her home life, from what little I knew of it, was less than ideal, but seriously, join the club. I was pretty sure Roxy had seen some fucked-up stuff go down at home, but she was doing all right. Roxy was shiny and bubbly and almost fantastical. She floated above us all like a mist—the shimmering contrail of a sarcastic fairy.

Roxy and I recognized each other right away. We were girls living out on the fall line, caught up in a current way stronger than we were, drawing us out to sea. Roxy and I didn't know each other very well yet, but we recognized each other as sisters. Then one weekend when we were away at lacrosse camp together, I could see something was eating her. I had never really seen her look quite that way before, so low energy and glum. I felt like I should try to talk to her. But what do you say to an unhappy unicorn?

"Is everything okay, Rox?" I asked lightly, flopping down on the end of her bed, trying to be present without invading her space.

"Yeah, I'm okay. Just life shit, you know." Roxy lay back against her pillow and stared at the ceiling. Then I think she may have sighed, a long exhalation of fairy dust that seemed to deflate her from the inside out. So, I did something very un-Southern and pried into her personal business without being invited.

"Are you sad about your dad?" I guessed, shocked that those words had come out of my mouth. Again, the South. We don't push. We'll give you all the time you need, all the time in the world. We don't expect people to broach difficult subjects until they're good and ready, which will hopefully be never.

Roxy's dad had passed suddenly around the same time as my mom did. It was easy for me to sympathize. I was going through the same kind of grief. To make matters even more

emotionally complex for her, Roxy's mom had surrendered custody. I guess in a way, when Ashley moved in, my dad did a
version of the same. I knew how she felt; I knew what it was like
to be uncomfortable in your own home, where you're supposed
to feel comfiest of all. I wanted Roxy to be able to talk to me
about that stuff, because more than maybe anybody else on the
planet, I got it.

"Yeah, I'm always sad about my dad," Roxy said. "You
know. That's just kind of a constant. But no, that's not it."

"Do you want to maybe talk about it?" I asked, because
I mean, when I'm feeling really upset about stuff, I don't like
to talk about it. I'm trying to work on that, though, because
talking about your feelings is just so much healthier. It's really
not good to bottle this stuff up.

"It's no big deal," Roxy said. "I just—I probably have to
move again. I gotta figure out somewhere I can go. I'm starting
to run a little short on open-ended invitations for places that
cost zero rent in Charleston."

"Well, when do you need to move?" My wheels were already turning. I needed an ally in the lunatic asylum, somebody
who was just exactly like my friend Roxy. She wasn't afraid of
anybody.

"Well, basically now," Roxy said, looking a little embarrassed. She was trying to be nonchalant about things, but I
knew that game.

"So where are you gonna go? Do you have a plan?" I asked.
And then very carefully, I touched the stove. "Can you go back
and live with your mom?"

"No, that's definitely out. But don't worry, Eva, I'll figure it out. Don't I always?" She looked fierce and invincible in that moment. Like a lady pirate.

"Well, we have an extra room at my house. I could call my dad and ask him if you could stay with us." I didn't want to sound too excited. I didn't want to spook her. People who are used to doing things on their own can get skittish when you offer to help. I'm like that. People trying to help me makes me nervous, but at the same time, it's exactly what I need. I wanted to help, but my dad could always say no. Normally, he would welcome anybody who needed a hand, no questions asked, but I wasn't sure he was that guy anymore.

"That's so nice of you, Eva, but wouldn't your dad get mad? I can't pay any rent or anything, but I'm great at cleaning the house."

"It's no trouble at all, trust me. I'd love it if you came and lived with us, and my dad is totally chill, you'll see. Ashley is, well, you can just ignore her. I do. I'll call him and see what he says. Okay?" Roxy nodded, so I went downstairs right away and dialed my dad to give him the 411.

"Sure thing, pumpkin. Of course Roxy is welcome to come and stay with us," my dad said, sounding like his sweet old self again just when I really, really needed him to. I almost did a cartwheel right there in the lounge but was afraid I'd take out the soda machine. "I'll come pick you girls up tomorrow. We've got plenty of room. It's the Christian thing to do. Poor kid."

I have to hand it to him. My dad walked his talk where his faith was concerned. He really meant all that stuff about doing unto others and extending a hand. My dad didn't always guess correctly about what God wanted from him, but he did his best to do the Christian thing. Meanwhile, I was so excited that I was going to have a friend under that fucked-up roof. And not for nothing, but on top of all her other features and benefits, Roxy was a full-on weed queen.

At first, I thought maybe Ashley would be happy about my having a friend living with us. This would let her have my dad and his worship of her all to herself. It was the next-best thing to me not being there. But I was wrong about that.

The very next day, my dad came and got us at lacrosse camp, and then we swung by where Roxy had been staying and picked up her stuff. I remember being shocked when all she came out with was a duffel and her camera equipment. But she spent her days defying gravity, so it made sense she'd travel light. When we got back to the house, Ashley was there waiting for us, looking all Christian and caring. She was way too hospitable and kind to Roxy. I knew right off what she was up to. Ashley was 100 percent trying to steal my friend before we even got inside the house.

As the days went on, Ashley moved in on Roxy like a king tide on a full moon. It was a full-on join-the-cult love bomb. So much for my ally in the house. Inside of a week, they were riding around town together in Ashley's ridiculous purple Cadillac that anyone with any sense would be embarrassed to drive. Roxy told me Ashley was preaching Trump and guns and God, trying to convert my ethereal, transcendent friend into some kinda troll under the bridge. Some people will just keep on eating, even though they're already stuffed to the gills. You couldn't leave Ashley alone in a room for fear she'd suck up the drapes.

I will say this for her: As with all gluttons for attention, Ashley can be very charming and alluring. She figures out what people want to see in her, and then she reflects that back, like a mirror on the wall, where Ashley is always the fairest of all.

CHAPTER 9

QUEEN OF A
THOUSAND THONGS

ey, kiddies, I'm home," I said, not as a greeting but as
a warning. I had made a habit these days of sounding
my horn before entering home port, just in case. But the harbor was empty. Thank God. Roxy had stayed at school after
practice to see her boyfriend, Sean. No sign of my dad or Ashley. Sully came running up to me, tail wagging like mad, and
jumped up, put his paws on my shoulders, and covered my face
in dog spit. I felt grateful for Sully on the daily. He was always
happy to see me. Somebody had to be. I relaxed on my watch
and headed straight for the fridge. I had been thinking about
fruit literally the entire way home.

"Oh, it's you. Home so soon?" Ashley hissed at me from
the shadows like some creature from *The Lord of the Rings*. It
startled me, so I slammed on the lights, and there she was, artfully arranged on the kitchen counter like a platter of kipnips,
wearing only a thong.

"School was good," I said, trying really hard to ignore the obvious. I mean, in a situation like that, what else can you do? I'll tell you one thing: I had definitely lost my appetite for the banana I had been dreaming about all the way home. It was sitting in the bowl right next to Satan's playmate, and I wasn't getting anywhere near that fruit bowl now.

"I find clothes tho confining thometimes, don't you, Eva? Ethpecially in this heat." The lisp was back, and my dad wasn't even home. So weird. Ashley slid off the counter and opened the freezer, positioning herself right in front of the ice maker for maximum exposure. I felt bad for the ice cubes. "I just de-thpithe the heat here." Um, she's from Florida. "Don't you just wish we could just free ourselves and never wear clothes at all?"

"I like clothes," I said. "Cute clothes are one of the only reasons I get out of bed in the morning. And it's March." Because I mean, for real? What was she going to do in July? And not for nothing, but Bradenton, Florida, is nobody's Alaska. The conversation ended in non sequitur, as it usually did. Ashley grabbed a tub of sliced cantaloupe, opened it, and began devouring chunks of the stuff, her fingers drippy with off-season goo. It was clearly August in Ashley's mind, even down to the snacks. That melon must have cost a bundle, too. Likely had to ship it all the way up here from Ecuador. Probably tasted like ass.

"You know what your problem is, Eva? You have body shame," Ashley told me, again apropos of nothing at all. "Your mom probably did, too. I'll bet she did, didn't she? Melon? I just cut it this morning."

"I'm all set, but thanks, Ashley. I gotta go for a run and then hit the books. Trig test tomorrow. Yikes!" I made a dash for the stairway to heaven, and my door, which had a lock on the inside.

"Aren't you going to ask me how my day went?" Ashley followed me up the stairs, running her sticky fingers along my mom's glowing burl maple banister. I had been so close to a clean getaway. It occurred to me then that she had been poised naked on that counter waiting for a reason. That after-school piece of performance art was meant for me. She was feeling some kind of way about something I'd done or not done, and now she was going to tell me all about it. Topless.

"How did your day go, Ashley? Did you have a nice time with your colored pencils?" I turned abruptly around on the stairs to face her. It startled Ashley, I could see that. I saw the fear flicker in her eyes for a moment. For once, a genuine, un-calculated moment. I watched her gather a spine, built out of fake outrage.

"My day was just fine until I saw the Amex bill this month, little Miss Eva." I noticed that her nipples were standing up like two exclamation points. Her blood was up and she was primed for battle.

"Look, Ashley, I don't want to argue with you, okay? It's stupid. Whatever it is you're upset about, you're right, it's all my fault. I'm sorry, I didn't mean it, and I'll never do it again, okay?" I knew very well by then that scrapping with my dad's naked Barbie dream bride on a staircase was a zero-sum game. I also understood that I was required to ask for no conflict only one time before engaging in self-defense.

"Did you really need two pairs of new pants at Lululemon, Eva? Don't you already have twelve?" This was rich coming from the queen of a thousand thongs. Roxy and I had gone through her drawers, and we found literal mountains of lingerie, and nothing else. She had bustiers and balconettes, camisoles and chemises, tap pants and thongs. It was like Victoria's Secret threw up in her drawers. She had every color in the porn rainbow.

"I don't remember seeing your name on my dad's credit card," I said, because I mean, come on, my dude, what the hell? It was none of her business what I spent my dad's money on. Retail therapy was a big part of how my dad helped me self-soothe after my mom's death. I'd shop during second-period biology and send my dad a pic of my cart. By the time I hit fourth-period algebra, my dad had given me the thumbs-up and transferred the money into my account, no questions asked. Was I spoiled? Maybe a little. But I didn't take advantage. I knew we weren't rich. I knew this was a way my dad could help me feel a little better. And it did help make me feel better, when almost nothing could make me smile.

And not for nothing, but Ashley hadn't worked a single day since my dad brought her to Charleston, and I know she was supposed to have found at least a part-time job. Wasn't she like Miss Big something or other in the Trump campaign? Didn't she think she was headed for the West Wing? She had to have some skills. I mean, besides writing on sticky notes with colored pencils and emasculating my dad. Maybe if she had found something to do. She might have made a friend. She might have been able to give my poor dad five minutes to himself. Things might have turned out completely differently.

"That's exactly what I have been telling your dad right from the start," Ashley said. "You have an attitude, young lady, and I don't appreciate your snark. Honestly, Eva, all I've done is try to be kind to you, try to be your stepmom, and all you do is sass back. You're not grateful for the blessings God has bestowed on you. I've been talking to your dad about that invitation from Roxy's aunt to go to Indiana. I think Christian ministry might be a good idea this summer after all. Maybe they can teach you to be more Christlike. Lord knows your father and I have failed at that."

I visualized launching into a flying tiger kick, sending her soaring over the newel post. Instead, I pushed past her and went downstairs, grabbed my backpack from the hook, and headed out the door. "I'm going for a run," I said. "And the next time you want to talk to me about something, put on a bra. I know you have like fifty." Then I let the door hit me where the good Lord split me. I knew she'd tell my dad that I'd been a brat as soon as he got home, and then my Lululemon privileges would definitely be suspended. But it was worth it.

Of course, when I got home a couple of hours later, there they were, arranged in their mom-and-pop chairs in the front room, pretending to be parental, but really just waiting to pounce. Then I was forced to endure a three-hour-long family meeting listening to my dad and Ashley lecture me about accountability and Christian values while I stared hollow-eyed into the abyss. My Amex privileges were put on an indefinite hold.

After that, I stopped bringing friends home from school. Absolutely none of my boys were ever allowed to come by. I mean, my God. Can you imagine? I tried to talk to my dad about it, but he was like, "Well, just rise above, Eva. That's how she's comfortable in her own home." Eventually, I started spending a lot of time in my room or in the art studio at school learning how to draw on the computer, or hitting the chronic hard with Roxy. I also leaned into the lacrosse team so I could stay at school as long as possible, until my dad got home from work.

There's always a bright side, I guess. I was getting really good at drawing, and I loved my art teacher, and I was feeling really fit and physically healthy. And also, being forced into getting serious about team sports at Wando made me realize that physical exercise really helped with anxiety. I was sleeping better. I had fewer nightmares. I felt less triggered overall. I loved playing lacrosse.

Playing sports taught me a lot of important stuff, like trusting my team and focusing on achieving a common goal. I learned discipline and determination. Resilience. And I placed second in the emerging new artist contest at school. I thought, *You see, Eva? When you take the initiative and make positive choices, rather than letting events control you, things work out better in the end. And even when you can't count on anybody else, not even your dad, now you're learning you can always count on yourself.*

During my whole sophomore year, my year of living dangerously, I was devoted to two things: lacrosse and my art. And then all summer long, it was me and my beautiful gray-green ocean, and my friends. Taylor and Vanessa and Sadie and Roxy were always by my side. And my boys Henry and Trent and Luke and Matty and Miles. My very own band of merry, swaggering, half-baked but completely glorious pirates.

But I still had to go home every day eventually, and that was always a whole Barnum and Bailey's worth of crazy. I'd just try to chill, watch Bob Ross, or listen to my music and paint until I could fall asleep. I went to bed with the sun like a farmer so I could get up and out early and run on the beach before school. I was running from the devil, but I got into the best shape of my life.

I didn't count on my dad anymore. I guess that's natural. I was trying to grow up as fast as I could because I knew my dad was never going to be able to clap back at Ashley. He would not intervene. I think my dad thought that he could fix Ashley. She was his project, and he couldn't give up on her. He thought his love could heal her. He thought that was what God wanted him to do, proving my point that grown men, even fathers, can still be idiots, too.

I was only sixteen, but even I knew that you can't change people. Not unless they want to change. And then they have to do that for themselves. Your love is not enough. And damage is not an excuse for being an asshole. Sometimes an asshole is just an asshole. In cases like this, it's best just to face facts and get off the porch before the shooting starts.

People around town knew that things were a little odd at home for me. I could tell people were worried. I made a point of avoiding the subject. I found it kind of upsetting to talk about it all. I kept it light, like I always do. Nobody pushed me. That would not have been polite. But I could tell they were on my side by the way people looked at Ashley. Their eyes were saying, "That girl is not from around here. I do not know her people, and I do not want to. Poor Eva!"

Nobody but nobody wanted to broach the subject of Ashley with my dad. He wasn't open to the possibilities on that subject. A few of his best friends, Mr. Wilson and Pastor Dan, and even my Uncle Dave had tried to talk to him about her. But my dad just shrugged things off or got defensive. He was in love. You can't reason with people who are in love unless you have an appetite for destruction.

I think it was around Easter that I started hearing Ashley and my dad talking about their ballet. At first, it was supposed to be just a little dance school to give Ashley something to do. About a week or two later, though, I realized that this little side hack to give Ashley a place to teach a ballet class for kids had mushroomed into a national ballet company based out of Charleston, with a touring company, and a conservatory, and I think a dance-wear line, because something something God's plan.

I didn't pay much attention to either one of them by this time, to be honest, because A) it was always about Ashley, not my favorite subject, and B) people had been trying to start ballet companies in Charleston since forever, and those companies died quicker than mosquitoes riding the rear bumper of a bug truck, as far as I could tell. Not that I was paying attention to the ballet world. And apparently, neither was anybody else around here once your daughter was older than about eight.

By the time the magnolias blossomed on Mother's Day, this ballet company was all Ashley talked about. It had developed into a multitiered arts complex with global reach, and my dad was chiming in way more than was seemly. They both sounded delusional, feeding off each other's grandiosity. My dad was on the phone all the time when he was home, talking to anybody who would listen about how they were uberizing the ballet and how Ashley was changing the world and they were inviting just a few select early investors. Whatever. I peaced out right around the time the past-due mortgage notices started showing up in our mailbox. I knew it was only a matter of time now before the brakes locked up.

"Doug, Sugar Plum needs a larger per diem or she can't come to Boston for open calls. Her mom said they need at least another five thousand." Ashley said this to my dad over dinner one night like she was asking him to pass the salt. My dad just kept cutting his grilled chicken into tiny pieces without saying a word. I could see his masticatory muscles fanning and un-dulating. Then he said a word I had been waiting to hear for months. "Ashley," he said, "no." And then he said it again, only louder. "No." And then he spelled it. "Enn. Ohhh." I was like, *Oh my God, finally. I am so here for this.*

"Well, what am I supposed to tell them, then, Doug? I need Sugar Plum. She's our prima ballerina. She has to have symme-try and chemistry with the other dancers. How am I supposed to know if there's symmetry and chemistry if she's not there at the auditions?" Ashley stared dead-eyed at my dad, drumming her fingers on the table. This is a bad habit that would have horrified my mom. I would have gotten my knuckles rapped with the handle of the butter knife for a move like that toot sweet. I mean, you do you, but for God's sake, learn some table manners.

"The well's run dry," my dad said. I noticed then that he looked like hell. His hair wasn't combed. He was all rumpled and unshaven. My mom would never have allowed him to look like that. Ashley just kept on talking at my dad while he chewed his chicken. She would go on and on like this all the time. My dad would just nod and listen quietly. I don't know how he did it. Ashley could screw a subject to a wall like a human drill gun.

"I've already poured tens of thousands of dollars of my own money into this project," my dad said. "And a lot of other people's money, too, I might add." My ear grew like a foot. That did not math. Where did my dad get tens of thousands of discretionary dollars? I mean, I knew he did okay. He had a good job, I always had everything I needed, but still, it had always been a little tight at the end of the month. My mom used to worry about it. The house was my mom's from her first marriage. My dad didn't have thousands of dollars just sitting around waiting to fund a passion project at scale for Ashley. And who else was giving my dad money for this cockamamie idea?

We didn't live in some former plantation house on top of a hill. We didn't go sailing to Bimini over spring break like a lot of my friends. But I never felt poor or anything. And all my friends had boats I could go out on whenever I wanted, and Sadie had her house on the beach, so who cared? My life was a village, and inside my village, all my material wishes were fulfilled somehow. And the center of my village was, without question, the Brown Fox coffee shop, where I hung out on the daily. Everybody knew about people's bottom lines around here. My dad had good bones, but he was clearly a fixer-upper. I guess when you grow up in the part of Florida where the circus carnies go in the off-season, you don't get a good sense of what people with real money look like. Or how they spend it.

"You're being unreasonable, Ashley. You don't understand the value of a dollar at all. We're already way over budget. We're over budget times ten," my dad said. "I've explained this to you before. Many, many times. I'm not made of money. Tell Sugar Plum's mom she'll have to wait until more investors come in. If that means they can't come to Boston, then they don't come to Boston. You'll have to imagine the symmetry without her." My dad never clapped back like this at Ashley in front of me. This was brand-new and sparkly and sweet smelling.

"Tell her yourself, Doug, because I'm done!" Ashley started sobbing for no apparent reason and without producing a single actual tear. When the sobbing didn't work, she got mad. "I'm not going to be in the middle of this for one more second. It's not fair. I'm supposed to be the creative part of this team, and I haven't gotten to spend a single second being creative." Side note: The only work I ever saw her do for the ballet involved sticky notes and colored pencils. She had all the school supplies and none of the school. "YOU are the business end, Doug. I'm the talent. Get it straight. And I'm done trying to keep everybody happy around here because you won't do your job."

Uh-oh, I thought. I didn't know how it'd happen, but I just knew that somehow, in some way, this was going to wind its way round to being all my fault. I tried to disappear seamlessly into my chair before one of them remembered I was in the room. "Doug, be reasonable," Ashley cajoled. The rage and hysteria hadn't worked, so now she was trying to reason with him. It must have been confusing for him. He had the devil on his shoulder appealing to his better angels.

"We need Sugar Plum, Doug. She's a brand. We're not a brand yet. Not like that. She's an Instagram influencer; we can't grow the kind of visibility we need without her. I mean, how will we go viral? You do want to go viral, don't you? And I've already told *Dance Magazine* that she's coming, and they're sending a photographer just for her. They want to do a whole editorial spread on her down by the harbor. What am I supposed to say to them? I'll just be so embarrassed if she's not there. We need this break. Just make it happen, honey. I know you can make it happen. You'll find the money. Call one of those rich friends of yours—they'll give it to you."

"They've already given me plenty, honey. I can't ask again. Not yet."

"Well, I don't know how to do these things. I'm not a businessperson. You said you were the executive. That's why I made you the CEO of my ballet, so now, go do what CEOs do and, fuck, I don't know, Doug, just man up and fix this."

What I was able to decipher from this straight up lunatic exchange was that Ashley was feeling some kind of way about my dad's leadership role in a business I did not know until I was this many days old even existed. And apparently, said business was already way over budget before the first pointe shoe had hit the dance floor. That tracked. "CEO of what, exactly?" I asked very quietly, very demurely, very un-Eva-ly, trying my best not to trigger an avalanche but secretly hoping for one just the same, so long as it didn't fall on the Brown Fox or me. It didn't matter really how or what I said, though, if I'm being honest. Nobody listened to me. Not anymore. Not even one single syllable.

"I'm putting things in place as fast as I can, Ashley. Just try to be a little more patient. There's no reason to freak out. I've got everything under control." My dad was struggling to keep an even tone, not making any sudden movements. Back up nice and slow. When she was like this, my dad always went into stealth mode. Probably wise. There was a lot of flying shrapnel, even back then.

"It takes a little time to raise two million dollars in this town, my love. People in Charleston can be cautious. They're conservative, slow to unlock their wallets because they are big, fat wallets, sweetie. We'll get there. Folks just move at a gentler pace down here. You have to go with the flow. I can't push a river, now can I?"

"Gentle? These people aren't gentle. These people are savages." Ashley rose, wounded but regal, out of her chair, paused in fifth position, pirouetted once or maybe even twice, and then sashayed away in the direction of the kitchen. I heard the water in the kitchen sink turn on, then off. After a few more seconds, I heard the bedroom door slam.

"Dad? Everything okay?" I asked, wishing the way you wish on a shooting star that he'd tell me they were getting a divorce.

"Everything's fine, sweetie. Don't you worry about a thing," my dad said. He carried his plate to the sink. Sully followed him into the kitchen, hoping for scraps. "Everything is going to be just fine." I heard the tinkling of Sully's leash, the back door slammed, and Sully and my dad headed out into the night.

CHAPTER 10

COCK IT AND PULL IT

All through that springtime of 2017, my second semester of sophomore year, there was tension thick as pluff mud piling up between my dad and Ashley. Whenever they were in the same room, you could feel that something just had or was about to happen. Once June came around, Ashley's mood seemed to brighten, and she left her ballet frustrations behind and turned her attention to staging a big formal wedding reception for herself. Why not? The house was in shambles, the renovation was still incomplete, she was opening a national ballet without a budget. Why not throw a wedding into the mix?

It didn't really take a leap of the imagination to grasp how this whole wedding thing bubbled up in her brain. It's gown town central around here in June. You can't throw a stick without hitting a bride. I think all the prenuptial hoopla reminded Ashley of the wedding she never got to have when she and my dad eloped without telling anyone, including me. Ashley drove to the plate so quickly by telling my dad she couldn't have sex before marriage, she bypassed all the wedding swag. She had got what she wanted and discovered it wasn't enough.

I could tell Ashley was experiencing some serious FOMO, like she'd been cheated out of something she definitely deserved. And so, despite the fact that the past due mortgage notices had been arriving each month like clockwork, and despite the fact that they were uberizing the ballet on a wing and a prayer, a grand reception was planned to celebrate their bad romance.

My dad's best bud and one of his principal investors in a bunch of his companies, including the coffee shop, the tech company, and now the ballet, offered up his landmarked house on Chalmers Street for the grand event. Good thing, too. Every inn, lodge, bed-and-breakfast, or church hall is booked up down here at least a year out. Big shindigs like a wedding don't happen on a shoestring in Charleston. These are opulent affairs, years in the making. But as with all things, Ashley thought she was the one exception to the rule. Her mom, Alicia, was flying in from Florida and said she'd take care of the food. I was skeptical, because my dad had to pay for her flight.

I hadn't met Ashley's mother before, but I'd spoken to her on the phone a couple of times, and I could tell she already didn't like me. She sounded more like an Ashley stan than a parent. Plus, I was told I had to give her my room and bunk in with Roxy, which made me nervous, because Roxy and I were in the middle of yet another stupid fight over some stupid boy. And to be honest, Ashley had started to come between us.

It made me so mad the way my dad just offered up my one and only space in that hell house that felt safe, like it wasn't mine at all. It wasn't even a dialogue. I mean, we had a conversation, but he did both parts. He answered for me with the words he wanted to hear. It went something like this:

"Alicia will take your room while she's here. You can bunk in with Roxy. You don't mind, do you, honey? Of course you don't; you're a sweet girl. Thanks so much, darlin'. That's why I love ya. We'll see y'all later now, bye, gotta run." The end. I was wondering why Alicia, a grown woman with a grown daughter, a daughter who had already been married before, couldn't find a room in a town with literally hundreds of hotels to choose from. But then I remembered that my dad would probably have had to pay for that, too.

About a week before the royal reception, Ashley dragged Roxy and me down to the Gown Boutique to pick out our fits for the big day. I found a cute but still dressy romper that was very me, but Ashley wasn't having it. She wanted to drape me in yards of ugly and told me that wearing a romper to her wedding was disrespectful. I thought I looked cute. And it was in Ashley's color story. Grinch green.

Not to be a snob or anything. I don't like to overemphasize social parameters—I mean, you do you. But this was a cocktail party in Charleston on the water in June, y'all. It was gonna be hot as Hades when the devil is in town. That means you wear what we call *porch formal attire* down here. You know, sleeveless linen shifts, seersucker suits, and yes, jumpers. Thank you. I didn't see why I needed to get up like Meghan Markle to hang out on a porch in a heat wave. So gross.

My dad stuck up for me and bought me the jumper I

wanted. Roxy bought one, too, in solidarity. I thought, *Finally, I get to win something.* I know it was only a wardrobe choice, but it seemed like a big deal to me. As it turned out, it was a big deal for the bride also. Ashley didn't speak to a single one of us for days. Then one night, just two days before the wedding reception, I came home from the beach, and the second I walked in the house, I knew something was wrong. Sully was lying in the corner of the kitchen looking guilty. My dad was sitting at the kitchen table with his head in his hands.

"Everything okay?" I asked. "You look shady. What happened?"

"I made a terrible mistake, Eva," my dad said without looking at me. Then he pointed up at a bloopy-looking bubble in the kitchen ceiling by the pot rack while still staring at his shoes. It wasn't a very big hole. Just a little round BULLET-SHAPED FREAKING HOLE in the ceiling. I felt a pit in my stomach.

I was used to guns in our house growing up. Everybody has guns down here. Everybody, unless you're a total fry. But our guns were always safely stowed and carefully handled, and both my dad and I knew how to use them. So did Ashley, for that matter. She had about four sidearms and a concealed carry permit. My dad was very strict about gun safety. You follow the rules. No exceptions.

"Did you get in a fight with Ashley?" I looked at the Glock on the table. It was Ashley's gun. "Is she . . . . dead?" I asked, holding my breath.

"Ashley's fine. Don't be so dramatic. Nobody's dead," my dad said, rubbing both eyes with the heels of his hands. That's when I looked at that hole again and realized that the kitchen ceiling was also the floor of Roxy's room.

"Where's Roxy?"

"Out with her boyfriend," my dad said. "Everybody's fine, Eva. Relax." Now that I knew nobody was dead, I started to feel a little judgy. I mean, my normally low-key navy pilot father would never discharge a weapon in the house. And certainly not in the midst of an argument. It went against everything he had taught me about, well, everything. Stunts like this were strictly against the Benefield Cider House Rules.

"You guys need to get it together or somebody is going to get hurt, and it probably won't be either of you two fools," I said sort of half under my breath, but he heard me, and he got a really hurt look in his eye, which made me feel bad. I admit, I was being disrespectful. I didn't want to hurt his feelings. He was under enough stress. But what did he expect? This constant role reversal was making me dizzy. I had been switching from kid to parent to kid again with like no notice. It was too much. It was all happening too fast. And I was sick of it. I had to pull the emergency brake.

"Do you have any idea what I go through for this family?" my dad said, moved by the depth of his own angst. He sounded like he was feeling very sorry for himself. Reminded me of somebody else I knew. Who was that again? Oh yeah. "I'm tearing myself to pieces trying to keep everything together for all of you. Have some respect. I'm doing my best."

"Was this fight about me?" I mean, I don't even know why I asked that—I already knew the answer. Of course it was about me. It was always about me. I was the only person in my dad's life that he refused to give up for Ashley. I was THE bone of contention.

"She found your diary," my dad said. "She read where you wrote that you hated her. She got upset. Understandable, wouldn't you say?"

"Wait, she read my journal? Did you just say to me that Ashley went into my room, and snooped through my things, and found and then read my journal? And that's okay with you? Real nice, Dad."

"She saw that you'd thrown away the little shadow box she made for you. She got her feelings hurt. She went off. You know how she gets. She put so much love into making that for you, Eva. You don't really hate Ashley, do you?"

My dad sounded so pathetic, I wanted to just run right out of the room and slam the door. But I was stuck on the fact that Ashley had read my journal. My dad didn't seem to notice me standing there, frozen in place, with my mouth hanging open. He just carried on our conversation, filling in the blanks for me with the stuff he wanted to hear. "Of course I know you don't hate her. It takes some time; you just lost your mom. I told her you don't hate her; you're just trying to get adjusted. I told her that, but she just kept on saying *Eva* this and *Eva* that. I got frustrated. Then I saw her gun sitting on the counter, and I just grabbed it and fired a shot into the ceiling. I thought it would make her stop."

"How'd that work out?"

"Well, it is a lot quieter now," he said, and we both tried

really hard not to laugh. I heard the back door slam, and Ashley stomped in, grabbed an apple, and macerated half of it into pulp in one bite, while staring daggers at the both of us. Then she went into the bedroom and slammed the door. Two days later, Roxy and I got all dolled up in our Grinch-green jumpers and headed off to the wedding of the century. Ashley's mother forgot to order the food, which, in South Carolina, is basically illegal. Poor Doc Darden had to run out to Whole Foods last minute and throw together a few party platters so we wouldn't eat each other.

Ashley and my dad arrived in a white stretch an hour and a half late. Ashley wore a basic-bitch ball gown with a beaded bodice and a full satin skirt that looked like it had been hauled out of some grandma's basement and put up for rent. I think it may have even had a train. We were all dying from the heat. Even in a jumper, I was like, *Jesus be a raindrop*. After the grand entrance, we all just sat around and waited for Ashley to melt into a puddle of satin poly.

Ben and Bev were a hard pass on the big day. Ben had been wounded on his last tour, and they were sticking pretty close to home. I didn't like to bother them with my problems. And ever since Ashley arrived on the scene, they were both completely disgusted with my dad. But I knew I could always call them in an absolute emergency. My brother John wasn't there either, which I couldn't blame him for. He said he couldn't take the time off work to come down from Tennessee. I looked around for Roxy, but she had snuck off to the carriage house to hook up with her boyfriend, Beau. When I turned back, Ashley was standing right in front of me. "You look beautiful, Ashley," I said, because frankly, I was scared.

"I don't want you in the formal family pictures," Ashley said. "That romper will ruin the portraits." Then Ashley and my dad made a toast to their future. After that, the other wedding guests—I counted eight of us, including Ashley's mother—and I sat around nibbling cubed gouda, counting the uncomfortable, irretrievable seconds until we could all go home, crank the air conditioner, and sleep it off.

CHAPTER 11

JESUS CAMP

Toward the end of July, Roxy and I were hiding upstairs watching a movie when Ashley and my dad moved in like a summer rain falling out of a cloudless sky. Completely unexpected, inexplicable, and unwelcome. They were all "knock, knock" and came in on tiptoes without waiting to be invited, like they were a couple of mischievous kids, all giddy and Lemony Snicket. They obviously had some insidious secret they were just dying to inflict on me. I was thinking, *Not tonight, Satan.*

"What? What is it now?" I asked them. Whatever was making my dad and Ashley giggle and blush like that, I knew it had to be heinous. I mean, couldn't I have just one day without some supernatural thriller unfolding in my bedroom? Was that asking too much of the universe?

"God hath truly blessed us," Ashley said. I noticed the lisp had returned. "It'th a miracle, girls. God hath anthered our prayers."

"What? Just tell me." I couldn't bear the suspense for one more instant. I just wanted to get it over with. And I hated that Ashley was making me invest so much energy into this phony and obviously scripted Q and A, which I knew had nothing to do with me and everything to do with manipulating my dad into whatever it was she wanted this week.

"You are going to have a little thister, Eva," Ashley said, dimpling and wrinkling up her nose like an evil cherub. The thought of Ashley becoming an actual mom made my blood run cold.

"She's going to be born right around your birthday." My dad said this like this was good news. "Maybe she'll wind up sharing the very same birthday as her big sister. Wouldn't that be something?"

I immediately broke into tears. My dad looked confused. Roxy looked terrified. Ashley was glowing.

No question. I was having a full-blown panic attack right in the middle of their gender reveal. I mean, what the hell? They hadn't even been married a year yet. My dad had only had his vasectomy reversed like, what, five seconds ago? It was supposed to take at least six months to a year before something like this could happen. And now, five seconds later, kaboom! Nuclear winter. I swear, I have the worst luck.

"Maybe we should give Eva a moment to calm down," Roxy said, watching me dissolve into heaving, hysterical sobs. Roxy hugged me close like my dad should have and didn't. Ashley rolled her eyes, crossed her arms, and shook her head like, *There she goes again. What an ungrateful brat. She's not even happy about having a baby sister on the way.* My dad took mercy on me and pulled Ashley out of the room. Roxy got up, kicked the door closed, and pushed the knob, which locked with a soft click.

"What are we going to do now?" I asked Roxy. It was more of a rhetorical question to the universe, so I didn't expect an answer, but Roxy was right there with a workaround.

"What do you think we're going to do? We are going to 420 the shit out of this ratched crap, get blasted beyond redemption, and hope that in the morning, when we wake up, this will all have been just a bad fever dream."

"But they'll smell it. We'll get in trouble," I said through my snot. "Ashley can smell a mouse fart from a mile off." Roxy smiled like the Cheshire cat and pulled out a pipe made out of an empty toilet paper roll. There was a Bounce sheet fastened to the end with a rubber band. See what I mean? Roxy was a weed genius.

"We'll bounce the smoke right past them," Roxy said, and torched up the toilet paper bowl right there in bed. Then we smoked our faces off all night long with the window open, watching the huge clouds of our exhaled smoke billowing out into the suburban night air, mingling with the humidity, becoming a ghost of the heat.

Ashley was in a chipper mood for about a week after the big announcement. Then she started in complaining about morning sickness and moping around the house looking Grinch greener than usual. It all seemed pretty over the top to me, but what did I know about being pregnant?

She was back on the sending Roxy and me to Christian ministry jag, and I wasn't having it. I had no intention of leaving my mother's house or my father's side, and I swore up and down that I'd have a massive panic attack and just die right there in front of her if she made me. So far, I was holding the line, but I could tell she wasn't going to relent, and something had to give. And then it did, the day my goldfish Cheez-It died.

Cheez-It was my goldfish that Roxy and I picked up at the county fair. Cheez-It had a twin named Cracker. We bought them together, and Roxy mostly took care of them. I mean, I'd feed them occasionally, but Roxy was the primary caretaker. She cleaned the fishbowls, looked after them on the regular. Roxy was good about stuff like that. Consistent care and whatnot. I was good in bursts, like my dad.

The night of Cheez-It's final exit, I was staying over at Sophie's. Roxy was out with her new boyfriend, Lincoln. Then about 9:00, my dad called me sounding all damaged and butt hurt. I could tell Ashley was yanking his chain about something I did or did not do. I could also tell my dad didn't really want to be calling up and yelling at me, but Ashley made him do it anyway. This is how it was now. Tag, Eva, you're it. Every single time.

"Eva, come home right now. Ashley and I need to talk to you," my dad said, sounding gruff. I could hear Ashley right next to him, egging him on. I rolled my eyes, thinking, *Oh my Lord, y'all, what now?*

"Am I in trouble?" I asked. "Because it sure sounds like I am." And honestly, wasn't I always? It wasn't a huge leap.

"Come on home now, Eva, and we'll talk about it when you get here. I don't want to do this over the phone," my dad said. And then for some reason, I knew instantly what Ashley was up to.

"I told you, I'm not going to Christian ministry with Roxy, so you can tell Ashley to lay off and get used to the fact that other people exist." I was fed up. This ministry idea of hers was going to be my Fort Sumter. I would not surrender. I would fight this to the last cannon. There was no freaking way I was going to Indiana to hang out with a bunch of other unwanted teens and talk about salvation. Not on your life, sweetheart.

"I'm not discussing this with you over the phone, Eva. Just come home now or I'm taking your car. And your phone." Then my dad hung up on me, something I don't think he had ever done before. What were my options at this juncture? I had none. I was still a kid. He held the title to my car. Paid for my gas. My phone was on his account. Push had come to shove; I had to go home. But I wasn't going to any Jesus camp. No, sir.

When I pulled up, the house was dark. I collected my-self and walked inside. My dad and Ashley weren't anywhere around. I heaved a huge sigh of relief and tiptoed up to my room, shutting the door silently, praying they hadn't heard me. I turned on the light in my room and realized, in a moment of what I can only describe as sheer terror, that everything—and I do mean everything—in my room was covered in Ashley's personalized heart-shaped pink Post-it Notes.

Ashley's sticky notes were the most horrifying Post-its on the planet—artificially cheerful and tacky and literally wallpapering my entire crib. It was stalker-level spooky. There were Post-its on my bed, on my dresser, and even on Cheez-It's fishbowl. There were notes on my pillow, on the mirror in the bathroom, inside the shower, and even on the toilet lid. I am not even kidding. And every note said the same thing, written in Ashley's loopy burn book Lucida font.

Eva, if you don't clean your fishbowl like I've been asking you to do for 4 days now then we're going to take away your fish and your phone.

Love, Ashley and Doug

I took a picture of my Post-it-papered room for Instagram, because in a situation like this, if there's no pic, it didn't happen, because nobody would believe it without un-pixelated proof. Next, I took the fishbowl and dumped the whole thing, Cheez-It and all, into the toilet and flushed. Then I put the empty fishbowl right back in its place. I know. I still wince when I think about it, but my dad had always taught me you fight the war you're in, not the one you wish you were in. I was involved in a war of mutually assured destruction. So, if the phone and the fish were leverage for the enemy, then I had to let them go. I'd let it all go. In fact, I already had. Except for my dad. A week later, Ashley scrubbed out Roxy's fishbowl with detergent, and Cracker died, too, in the residue from the Dawn.

I had let a lot of things slide since that day my dad waltzed in and announced he'd married Ashley. I had watched my entire world, everything that I had ever depended upon for a sense of safety and security, get disassembled like an IKEA desk. Now my mom's bright, cheerful home was painted black. All of her cute and tasteful accents went out with the trash. Fine. So be it. My memories of my mom lived in my heart, and the rest, whatever. But this, I didn't forgive. I swore that for as long as I lived, I would never forget the day that Ashley turned me into a killer of fish.

The next day, Roxy and I were ordered into a family meeting, and all our weed paraphernalia was laid out in neat little rows on the dining room table. There were heart-shaped Post-it Notes stuck to everything that said this in Satan's careful script:

PACK YOUR BAGS YOU'RE GOING
TO CHRISTIAN MINISTRY,
Jesus Saves ❤

And so, two weeks later, Roxy and I were on a bus to Jesus camp. Roxy seemed excited. She said farm boys from Indiana were hot, and it was her aunt's invitation in the first place, so she had to own it. I was outraged. And mortified. When we arrived, there were about eight hundred of us misfit toys, all crammed into a Baptist chapel in some Podunk burg fifty miles north of Gary, Indiana. We hung out listening to Christian Coldplay and tried to feel saved. Roxy hooked up the first night with a boy from Boulder. We both went home with lice.

CHAPTER 12

THE SUGAR PLUM FAIRY
IS FOR SUCKERS

I stayed mad at Ashley and my dad for a long time after Cheez-It's untimely demise. That sacrifice changed me. I started thinking more like a lady pirate. I vowed revenge. I plotted and planned and trimmed my sails until the time was right. And then, when my moment finally came, I went full tilt into the wind's eye. There was no going back for me now.

I had noticed that Ashley had put out a little bowl of jellybeans on the kitchen counter. Ashley said she'd had a craving for them ever since she got pregnant, and she would pick at those jellybeans all day long. So one night, when Ashley and my dad were out, I took the jellybeans out of the bowl and let Sully lick every single piece of candy. Then I put them back in the bowl and watched Ashley eat every doggie bean. I didn't even feel bad about it. It felt like power. It felt like justice.

It was pretty bouncy around the house by then. Especially for my dad. Ever since Ashley got pregnant, she'd become completely unpredictable and often morose. You never knew which Barbie you were going to get. I could handle moody Barbie; she was quieter. But over-the-top chipper and happy Barbie really freaked me out. Like the Barbie who came in chirping like a bluebird about a reality show, right at the beginning of my junior year.

"You'll never guess what's happened, Eva. It's the most exciting thing ever." It was the first thing in the morning. I'd been out pretty late with Sadie and Matty at a bonfire on the beach the night before. All I wanted was coffee and a quick exit. Ashley's eyes were sparkling with some kind of strange brew, though, and I was realizing that a grab-and-go was off the table. I had to spend a few moments basking in her lunatic light or else.

"You know your dad and I have been working so hard with the dancers arriving soon." I was thinking, *Lalalalalalalalala,* because I had told them both that I did not want to hear anything more about that damn ballet. It was triggering. And super toxic. I didn't want that ballet to come into contact with any exposed skin.

"Breaking news!" Ashley warbled. "We're working on a big deal with some big producers in Hollywood for a reality show about the dancers. They said HBO is interested, Netflix, Apple, Hulu—everybody. I mean, just everybody. Eva, if you're good—I mean, if you're really, really, really good—I'll even let you be in it."

"That's cool. Thanks, Ashley," I said. Ashley smiled and flipped her hair, causing a waterfall of artfully layered and coconut-conditioned brown locks to launch and land perfectly around her shoulders. I have to give it to her. Girlie has great hair. She took a big bite out of a slice of watermelon. I watched the red juice trail down her chin and plop onto the pile of dancer's headshots on the table with a sloppy splat.

"Your dad and I—we are going to change the world with this ballet," Ashley said. She finished the melon, chucked the rind, and grabbed a fistful of jellybeans from the bowl on the counter. Sully watched her intently, licking his chops.

"How can a ballet school change the world?" I wondered aloud. Once again, questions I did not really want to know the answer to. But she was talking about a ballet, right? It wasn't a global initiative to fight climate change or child hunger or anything.

"Your dad understands how important this work is, to create an inclusive ballet," Ashley said. "I mean, obviously he does. He's earmarked two and a half million of his own personal dollars to launch this project. Our prima, the too-tall Sugar Plum Fairy, arrives next week, and the rest of the corps will follow at the end of September. I was a too-tall Sugar Plum Fairy myself once, did you know that, Eva? And yet, look where I am now!"

I wondered where she thought she was exactly that warranted all that self-congratulation. I wondered if her neck was sore from kissing her own ass. Then I was like, wait . . . WHAT? Did she just say two and a half million of my dad's personal dollars? My dad did not have two and a half million dollars. My dad didn't have twenty-two dollars last week when I needed money for lunch. Where did Ashley get the idea that my dad had guap like that? Doug Benefield wasn't a zaddy. He was no patron of the arts. I doubted he could even spell *ballet*. And a person did not look at Ashley and think, *Wow, there goes a future founder of an international arts organization.* For me, it was more like, *There goes a future waitress at that dive out on Route 9, where the servers wear bikinis and you don't have to check your gun at the door.*

And in case anybody—and by *anybody*, I mean Ashley—might have forgotten, there was now a baby on board. My little half sister. A real, live human baby that did not know how to take care of herself while Ashley and my dad uberized ballet and made reality shows with a bunch of too-tall Sugar Plum Fairies. Ashley stretched her leg up over her head in a Gumby move that she pretended was effortless. We both knew it wasn't. Neither one of us cared.

"We're going to be an inclusive and diverse company at ANB, did I tell you?" She had. Repeatedly, and also, like, five seconds ago. "We will be hiring alternative dancers and giving everyone a chance to dance for the glory of our heavenly father. We will be God's ballet." Ashley put her right leg down and pulled the left one up, almost taking out the overhead light. An overhead light my mother would have hated.

As I watched Ashley twist herself into a tortured arabesque, I wondered, how did she settle on the ballet thing anyway? You could tell Ashley had taken a lot of dance classes. Her movements were precise, and she was superstrong and yet still lithe, even willowy. But it wasn't beautiful to watch her. She wasn't graceful. Her movements were joyless. Who, I wondered, was the person who should have told her this years ago and didn't? Who was it that could have led her in a better direction, where she might have found real fulfillment and saved us all a lot of heartache?

I texted my friend Taylor a desperate SOS. My whip was in the shop, and I was stranded until somebody came and peeled me off the premises. Ashley kept talking. And talking. And talking. She was good at that. Inexhaustible, really. Now she was on about that ballet person my dad had brought in to do the job Ashley wasn't doing. I had met her only once, the day she hit town. She already looked confused. Well, she had landed right in the middle of a Southern deep-fried cluster fuck. "And you know that strange older woman Bettina something, you know who I mean, your dad brought her down from New York, or was it DC, or LA? No, Austin. Well, whatever. I thought she was very odd. Is it just me? Have you met her? Your father thinks the sun rises and sets on her. I don't see it, but she is bringing in some famous dancers from New York so the donors will take the padlocks off their wallets. It's all about the money now, isn't it, Eva? So sad when that happens. Don't you wish we could just live and dance and never worry about clothes or money ever?"

My friends often tell me they're surprised I didn't turn out to be a heroin addict. All I can say is I'm in my own world a lot, and there's safety and even a kind of beauty in that. It's almost an art form. I began perfecting my craft the day I lost my mom. For the most part, I stay positive and focused on the things you're supposed to care about when you're in high school—finding a boyfriend who isn't an idiot, and stopping Roxy from moving in on every boy I think is cute. I stayed on top of my carb score. My carbon footprint. Passing trig.

I try to keep it real, though. I don't pretend everything is all puppies and rainbows when it's not. My friends get that about me. I can be who I am with my squad. I don't like fake sweet, and you see a lot of it down here. Like the Sugar Plum Fairy. I have been triggered by the Sugar Plum Fairy since I was little. I am suspicious of anyone with a hard candy coating. I know that underneath all that sugary crunch, a sugarplum is just a moldy piece of fruit that has probably been licked by a dog and then put back in the bowl.

Later that week, my dad came walking in the back door unzipping a duffel bag full of cash slung over his shoulder. There must have been like fifty, sixty grand in there minimum, all in small bills. I had gotten pretty good at keeping my powder dry (see: everything up to now), but when something like this goes down right in your front room, you feel like maybe you ought to say a little something.

"What's up, Dad? Did you get a second job as a mule for the cartel?" I snickered. It was nervous laughter. I do that sometimes. Dark humor is my mac and cheese. My dad normally would have thought my joke was funny. Not that day. I don't think he even heard me. He was focused on whatever petty larceny he may or may not have been committing.

"Sugar Plum and her mom are flying in tomorrow, and there are a whole bunch of dancers flying in right behind her. I don't have my checks from the bank yet on our new account, so

I have to pay them all in cash, no big deal. I got this. Always a little bumpy in the beginning of these big, new ventures. Everything's gonna be just fine," my dad said with seriously delulu-level confidence.

"How much money do you have in there?" I asked. My dad let the strap slide off his shoulder. The duffel bag fell onto the dining room floor with a dull thud, like a dead body.

"Fifty grand," my dad said, and started to count out the cash and slide it into little white envelopes. Then he labeled them each with one of Ashley's pre-addressed, heart-shaped pink Post-its. Those freaking notes were haunting me, turning up stuck to every next nevermore. "Don't take any pictures and post them on the internet, Eva. I don't want anybody knowing we have this kind of cash in the house." I'll bet. My dad had top security clearance with the government. For now.

"Where did you get that much cash, Dad?" Stupid question. I couldn't seem to help myself. Terrible habit.

"I told you; we brought in an investor." I stood there watching him count out his cash and stuff it into envelopes, labeled with those freaking heart notes, and I wondered if there was a specific day or hour when my dad stopped being a normal guy who went to work, came home, ate dinner, went to the beach with us on the weekends, cracked dumb dad jokes, and showed up at my lacrosse games to cheer me on or yell at the ref for making a bad call. That dad had been replaced with this guy with eyes in the back of his head and a duffel bag full of Benjamins slung over his shoulder.

I can't even explain how hard it is to watch someone you love that much change for the worse before your eyes and to not be able to do a damn thing about it. You try to tell them the truth, but they can't hear you over the lies they're telling themselves. My dad was running himself into a wall trying to make Ashley happy. But Ashley was never happy. In her eyes, my dad always came up short.

See what I mean about Sugar Plum Fairies? Rotten to the core.

CHAPTER 13

THINGS YOU SHOULD NEVER DO, JUST TO BE ON THE SAFE SIDE

☠ Never count your fish before you dock for the day.

☠ Never hang a horseshoe upside down.

☠ Never cheers with water in your glass.

☠ Never marry somebody you met two weeks ago.

☠ Never pick up a quarter that's tails up.

☠ Never sail into a red sky in the morning.

☠ Never start a ballet if you can't pay your mortgage. In fact, just don't start a ballet.

☠ Never pass up the opportunity to tell your mother, *I love you, too.*

☠ Never write a chapter 13.

CHAPTER 14

BUN ON THE RUN

As another autumn started its slow sprawl over the Low Country, I was getting ready for my junior year and a fresh start. I started by coming to terms with the fact that brewing espresso and steaming milk into velvety foam might be a viable future career path for me. I did love being at the Brown Fox more than just about anywhere else at the time. I loved the happy buzz of well-caffeinated folks munching scones, scrolling on their laptops, lifting up their faces to the Carolina sun peeking through the window, at the beginning or the end of their regular, routine, normal days.

I hated going home. I had to work myself up to walk back through those doors every single day. My dad looked like Ashley had plugged him into a wall and cranked his switch to eleven. I was just waiting for a breaker to blow. I tried to dial things down. Believe it or not, I can be quite anodyne when I want to be. I'd say things like "Let's go out just you and me, Dad. Give Ashley a little room to breathe." Or I'd say, "Maybe we could get up early and go fishing out on Sullivan's. Maybe grab a plate of wings at Dunleavy's after, like the old days. We don't have to talk about Ashley. I won't even bring her up. We can talk about other stuff."

Even when I could coax my dad out alone, it was awkward. So many uncomfortable silences. Ashley was such a big part of his life that, outside of her, he didn't have much to say. He knew and I knew he would catch hell from Ashley as soon as he got home. So, the whole experience would be full of menace and dread. I could tell he resented me for the rift, even though he knew deep down that it wasn't my fault.

Almost a year to the day exactly from that Friday I first met Ashley, I got home from school, and my dad was already home, looking squirrely. And Ashley's grape Kool-Aid zaddy caddy was gone from the driveway. I couldn't figure out how that could be. When I left for school that morning, Roxy had her parked in. How had this happened? What were the unnatural physics of this event? It was freaking me out. It's one of those moments when you realize that you've been living in a fun house, where the fundamental laws of the universe no longer apply.

"Ashley went to Florida," my dad said. His voice was kind of stuck in his throat. When he spoke, the words sounded like water trapped in a pipe. He was still trying to pretend like everything was fine. Maybe he really believed it was. Maybe he was that much of a fool in love. But that's hard to admit, even now. "She was having a rough time with the morning sickness—you know how she's been—and then all the added pressure with the ballet. I can't be here enough to take care of her, and we thought

it would be best if she went and stayed with Alicia for a while."
I was instantly bathed in relief. I felt hope again for the first
time since I could remember. If I had been a bell, I would have
been ringing.

It would have been a glorious moment, everything I had
been hoping for, were it not for my pathetic father, who looked
like he just lost his reason for living. I hated seeing my dad
vulnerable like this. It made me so uncomfortable, and I didn't
really understand why exactly. "Maybe it's for the best, Dad.
This will give you guys a chance to regroup. You guys can come
back together when you're both rested and refreshed. You want
a macchiato? I can draw your name in milk foam now; I've been
practicing." See? Now I was doing it. My family always goes to
caffeine in a crisis. The world will be coming to an end, and the
Benefields will be all, *Who's down for an Americano?*

"It was just too much for her. This damn ballet. I don't know
why she had to hire so many dancers. I mean, forty-five dancers
all descending on us at once. And then with the baby. It was just
too much. I should have seen it, slowed things down." This was
how it was with my dad and me now. Contrapuntal monologues.
Two ships, different lanes, chugging out to open water.

"Yeah, what about the ballet, Dad? I mean, she'll be back to
greet the dancers, right?" My dad shrugged in a way that said,
Nope, she's not coming back, but I'm not gonna say it out loud.
"We'll see" is what he eventually said. "The baby and Ashley's
health have to come first." He was now actually apologizing for
her in advance. Like he already knew and yet didn't know, all
at the same time.

"How are you supposed to handle all those ballerinas without Ashley? I mean, what are you going to tell them? You don't know anything about this. I mean, have you ever even seen a ballet?"

"Bettina is here. She'll handle all that. We're just going to take things one step at a time, and then Ashley will come back, and she'll have the baby, and we'll launch the ballet, and everything will be peaches, peaches." My dad got up, pinched my cheek, took my cup out of my hand, and finished making my macchiato for me. I wasn't sure what to say or do. It was a complicated situation. Too complicated for a sixteen-year-old girl who was majoring in milk foam. So I just drank my coffee and remembered that my mom used to tell me, *Sometimes all you can do is love somebody, Eva.* So that's what I did. I loved him.

I was pretty sure right then and there, after listening to my dad lie to himself so unconvincingly, that Ashley wasn't ever coming back to Charleston. Yet in a moment when I should have felt incredible relief that Ashley was finally out of my life, I felt the old panic rise up inside me like a shredder wave, ready to top the levee.

CHAPTER 15

LAST DANCE

On September 18, 2017, all the Instagram ballerinas Ashley had hired over the internet flew into Charleston with heads and hearts full of Insta promises of a full year's contract, a pointe shoe budget, and full medical coverage. Plus a housing allowance. None of this was true. Of course it wasn't. How many Insta ballerinas in the world get a deal like that? Zero, that's how many. It was all just a bunch of Ashley's Insta lies. But the Insta ballerinas didn't know this. And Ashley wasn't there to tell them. She left that pleasant chore to my dad. And then my dad left it to Bettina.

My dad went off that morning with his sticky-noted envelopes of cash to greet the dancers. And while he was gone, Ashley came and loaded up her caddy with all her stuff and hightailed it back to Florida, and that was that. She left me a note: *I've taken the cats.* I found my dad sitting on the bed in his bedroom looking as heartbroken as the day my mom died.

Which kinda pissed me off, to tell you the truth. He had a letter in his hands, written on cheesy Hallmark stationery. What else? I recognized Ashley's creepy Hobby Lobby script. And there were a lot of pages mostly complaining about my dad, money, and the state of our indoor plumbing. That tracked.

It was pretty brutal for her to peace out on him in that exact moment and blame the dishwasher and the bathroom hot water faucet. And to choose that precise day, when she knew my dad would be busy covering her ass. It was twenty-four-karat Ashley. She didn't feel anybody's pain but her own.

I knew my dad was still telling himself this was only temporary. I knew he thought she'd be back before the baby was born, and I knew he was still madly in love with her, if love is what you would call it. I wasn't too sure about that. It felt more like addiction to me. Throughout that whole fall, my dad and his new best friend Bettina, who I had only met for like five seconds, were spending every moment together, working themselves up into a lather trying to bail out Ashley's sinking ballerina barge. But even I—I, who was trying not to pay attention—could see they were sinking into the kook soup. Then Hurricane Irma hit. My dad drove down to rescue Ashley and never came back. Bettina was left in Charleston to go down with the ship.

First, they laid off half the dancers, which caused a tulle bomb to explode in the dance press. Then Sugar Plum quit because she was mad about the other dancers getting fired. Finally, Ashley went on to the ANB Facebook page and annihilated what remained, along with all grammar and syntax.

A note from the founder
of the American National Ballet:

I want to start by saying that I publicly disavow my support for American National Ballet and its leadership.

I have been on personal leave and out of state since the end of August and heard second hand about the devastation that took place on October 23rd.

As the founder I am completely devastated by what has been done and the way it was done. The new leadership has destroyed all that we worked so hard to build and I can not stand behind them or their actions. ANB was created to be different from any other company and was supposed to set a new standard in how it treats its dancers. Everyone involved should be ashamed of themselves for how this was handled.

My heart goes out to all those affected by recent changes. Each and every dancer brought on possesses amazing talent and potential. The original group assembled was truly diverse in every way and this is a huge loss for America and for art lovers around the world.

As I am no longer associated with this organization in any way, please feel free to share your concerns with ANB's leadership.

Sincerely,

Ashley Benefield

One week later, the American National Ballet disappeared beneath the waves. My dad started spending most of his time in Florida, and honestly, it felt better and calmer being on my own. And when my dad was back in Charleston, things were getting better between us too. For one thing, Ashley wasn't around to cause friction. For another, the distance did us good. Still, I was pretty butt hurt, I'm not gonna lie. I didn't want to be mad at my dad, but I didn't know how to get un-mad at him. Then one day, he asked me a question and stopped talking and waited for me to actually answer in my own words.

"Eva, are you mad at me?" he asked, and because this was a rare opportunity that I wasn't sure would happen again, I leaned into the moment. Even though I knew he was still heartbroken over Ashley, and even though I knew he was vulnerable, I made the decision to tell him the truth. I thought it might be my last chance, and as it turned out, it was.

"I guess I am mad at you a little, Dad. You introduced me to Ashley two seconds before you married her. You didn't even invite me to your wedding. You totally forgot about me once she moved in, and you've never even said that you're sorry about any of it. I mean, I'm a person with social anxiety disorder. I had just lost my mother. I was having panic attacks on the chronic, and you didn't even care."

"Of course I care, Eva," he said, and tried to put his arm around me. I wriggled out of his embrace. I wasn't going to make it that easy for him, even though it felt really good to have my dad back, and I hoped it would last longer than a few seconds, even though I knew it probably wouldn't.

"No, you didn't," I said, and I was right about that, too. Extra right. "You didn't care, Dad. How could you when you didn't even have two seconds left over to pay attention to anybody except Ashley? You let her monopolize you twenty-four, three-sixty-five. All you thought about was Ashley, Ashley, Ashley. Admit it."

"You're right," he said. "You're right, Eva, and that was not fair of me, and I'm very sorry. I really am, sweetheart. And I hope that you can forgive me."

And that was all I needed. It's amazing how accountability and a sincere apology can make everything so much better. All my anger just evaporated like the dew. Such a simple solution that solved all the complex emotions I'd been feeling. Why had that been so hard? After that, I became instantly un-mad. My dad and I went back to talking about life and having dinner together, and sometimes we took day trips out on the boat, and he started making me coffee every morning and eggs sunny-side up.

With Ashley gone, I had been able to start having a life of my own. For one thing, I fell in love for the first time. Yes, I finally found a boyfriend who wasn't a total fry. In fact, he was kind of a catch. Tall and tan and sandy-haired and sweet. And a waterman, which is kinda hot. Pete was a low-key Low Country warrior, just like me. Just like my dad.

My dad listened to me go on and on about Pete, even though I know I must have sounded like a complete fool. "Why hasn't he texted me back yet? It's been five minutes. I know he read the text. Maybe he isn't that into me. Oh, wait! He just texted me back." My dad would just smile and shake his head, like he wasn't a guy swimming in the same deep ocean, clinging to text messages like our lives depended on it. And drowning.

"Give it time," my dad would say. "Don't be so impatient. Savor this time when you are just getting to know each other. Don't rush things. This is the fun part, pumpkin. Puppy love is the best, so relax and enjoy it. You're making memories you'll cherish for the rest of your life." In retrospect, this goes past ironic. Did he hear himself? He was right about the memories, though. To this day, whenever I think about falling in love with Pete, I smile.

Once Ashley moved to Florida, I didn't hear a lot about what was going on with the two of them. It was a shock to discover everything that had been happening down there later at trial. He had been telling me everything was fine. I thought things were settling down. I thought he was happy, and so I was happy. I wanted things to keep going just like they were, but I knew in the back of my mind that wasn't how things were going to unwind. Things would change. There was still a baby on her way.

In April, right around my seventeenth birthday, my dad told me he and Ashley were having problems. My dad was spending a lot more time in Charleston, and I didn't hear much about Ashley. I did kind of wonder: Shouldn't Ashley be having her baby soon? Wasn't she supposed to be born right around my birthday? Suddenly, I needed to know. Do I have a sister now that I haven't met yet? Did something go wrong? Is my dad hiding something? Has it all been a lie from the beginning? Maybe she went mad and threw herself into the Manatee River. Maybe my dad isn't the dad after all, and now Ashley is living with her real baby daddy and has given birth to their love child, and all of this will have been a mistake, and everyone will live happily ever after. Well, all of us except for that poor baby.

Then my dad told me that he and Ashley weren't speaking, and I let the sleeping dog lie. It wasn't until six months later, right around Halloween, that my dad told me I had a sister, whose name was Emerson. She had been born at the end of March. He told me he only learned about this from the papers Ashley served my dad trying to terminate his paternal rights. So this is when I started to get clued in to the real state of affairs with Ashley in Florida. My dad's name wasn't even listed on the birth certificate. No matter what was going on between them, this was a real cold play. Emerson deserved to know she was a Benefield. She deserved to know she had a great dad who loved her so much and wanted to be a part of her life.

Ashley had convinced the doctors at Tampa General to give her a C-section three weeks before her due date. She claimed my dad had poisoned her with heavy metals that he put in her pregnancy Teavana. They tested her for toxins at the hospital, but nothing showed up. Big surprise.

After that, things got super complicated for my dad. He had been telling me everything was rainbows and puppies down in Bradenton, but obviously, it wasn't. They started fighting over custody, and money was getting tight. My dad was paying for his lawyer, HER lawyer, three therapists, plus child support for a baby he hadn't even met yet. And he was still supporting Alicia and Ashley. Why he stuck by her like that, I will never understand. If he were alive today, I swear he'd probably still be defending her.

CHAPTER 16

SCARY MONSTERS

Just before Thanksgiving, I was home doing my homework (for once) when somebody came knock-knockin'.

"Miss Benefield? We're from CPS. Can we come in and talk to you for a few minutes, please, darlin'?" said a woman with shiny brown hair and glasses that were way too big for her face. She had let herself in through my open porch door and was peeking into the front room looking very judgy for somebody who had just shown up without an invitation.

"My dad's not home, ma'am," I said. "I'm sorry, but I'm not allowed to let strangers in the house when my dad's not here." I realize I sounded like I was five with the stranger danger thing, but I didn't want to answer a bunch of stupid questions from child welfare officials all triggered by what I was sure was another bogus abuse complaint phoned in by you know who. She was down there doing whatever she could think of to make my dad look bad in front of the family court judge who would decide the custody case. I knew what this was probably about, but it's still super alarming to have child welfare workers walk in while you're trying to conjugate French verbs.

The officials weren't in uniform, so did I technically have to let them in? Were they like law enforcement? Didn't they need a warrant or something? I wasn't sure. It felt like a gray area. The balding guy next to Nutresse held up a badge that looked pretty official, so I invited them in. What else was I gonna do? I was a sitting duck.

"We just have a few questions," CPS Nutresse said, nosing her way around the front room without taking off her shoes, which had been the rule around the house ever since my mom got the new oak floors put in. My dad and I had managed to restore the front room to a soft taupe by then, but the kitchen was still deep space.

"Make yourself right at home," I said, because they obviously already had. They didn't seem to pick up on my sarcasm. Every time I turn around these days, somebody is slaughtering irony. Bald guy plunked down in my dad's chair in the living room. He looked like his feet hurt. Nutresse sat down on the couch and smiled up at me in an understanding and semi-sisterly way. They both just stared at me for a while. I stared back.

"Eva, we're here today because we got a call from someone who's concerned about your safety and your welfare," she said.

"Let me guess: Ashley Benefield?"

A brief look of concern flitted across Nutresse's face. She was subtle, but she had a tell. I saw her left eye and upper lip twitch and I knew I had hit the bullseye.

She saw me see her, and quickly smiled. When she did, I noticed Nutresse was actually young and pretty underneath all that drab officialness. Her eyes were light as birchwood, with shots of gold that sparkled in the sunlight flooding in through the front window, where I'm sure my neighbors were watching and eating this up with a ladle. "Have you ever felt afraid of your father, sweetheart? Has he ever threatened you or hurt you in any way?" How's that for an icebreaker, right?

"No, ma'am. My dad has never hurt me. I have a great dad," I said, because it was 150 percent true. Nutresse did not, however, look convinced.

"What about the dog? Is your puppy afraid of your dad?" I could tell she was trying to sound very friendly and concerned, and perhaps she genuinely was. But she had some work to do on her approach. First of all, I wasn't six. Second of all, at least buy me lunch before you ask me if my dad is a violent abuser. Especially since he wasn't.

"I'm not even a little bit afraid of my dad, and neither is Sully." I tried not to sound too dramatic, which isn't exactly easy for a sixteen-year-old girl under investigation by the parent police. I didn't want them to think I was covering up anything or getting defensive. But it didn't seem like they were taking anything I said at face value. Not being believed when you're lying is annoying enough as a teenager, but when you're telling the God's honest truth and they don't believe you, it's completely maddening.

"My dad is not scary. Really. Nobody is scared of my dad."

The two of them didn't nod or smile. I don't think either one of them even blinked. They just sat there staring at me, letting the silence swallow us whole. I think they thought I'd fill in the gaps. But they would be wrong. "My dad and Sully are best friends," I said finally. "They go everywhere together."

It was really exasperating to have people thinking my dad, who wouldn't even hurt a fly, was violent or cruel. When my mom would see a spider and scream for my dad to come kill it, he'd say, "No, honey, those spiders eat mosquitoes and aphids. Every creature on God's earth serves a purpose. Circle of life, Renee." Then he'd carry the spider outside and set it free in the garden. This did not make my mom, who loved all living creatures except for spiders, very happy at all, but that's how he rolled. My dad respected all life. Even spiders. Even Ashley. Especially Ashley.

"You know she hasn't lived here for months, right? She just sits down there in Florida phoning in lies to make my dad look bad. She never tells the truth about anything. Like seriously never." I could see bald guy's wheels turning. He was thinking that this is just exactly the kind of attitude one expects from a troubled teen living in an abusive home like mine.

"We can't deny or confirm who called us," he said. "That's for your safety as well as the safety of reporters."

"And it's the law," Nutresse added with a little too much edge. She heard it and adjusted. "We all just want to make sure that you're happy and safe, honey. Where is your daddy today, Eva?"

"He's traveling on business." I said this and then realized

that maybe I should qualify that, since technically I wasn't legally old enough to be home alone yet even though I'd been taking care of myself for a while by then. But if they wanted to get nitpicky about things. Which they totally might. "He'll be home tonight. And my brother and sister-in-law look in on me while he's away. And Melanie across the street does, too." Nobody had to look out for me. I was seventeen years old. Practically a grown-up. CPS nodded in concert. "I see, I see," they said in a way that made me 100 percent sure that they didn't see at all. In their defense, how could they? I mean, my situation was complicated.

I was never really alone in Mount Pleasant. I mean, not really completely on my lonesome. I lived in a small village; it felt practically colonial, and everybody knew me. Everybody knew everybody since like birth. People minded their own business for sure—it's the South—but they were there just the same, watching, making sure I didn't crash into a wall or get into any serious trouble. If that had happened, somebody would have stepped in, or at least I thought they would. I never found out, though, because I didn't crash. I was fine on my own. I wanted to do my life by myself, because I knew that I could probably do a much better job at it than the adults in my life were doing.

Plus, I had Pete, my quiet, low-key waterman, who loved the ocean like I did and was an excellent sailor and always had my back. CPS finally packed up their kit and said they'd be in touch and left. We didn't hear anything from them for a while. I half hoped that would be the end of things. Maybe they figured out Ashley was crazy and closed the case. But then a few weeks later, the whole entire Mount Pleasant police department wound up on my doorstep.

"Hello there, Miss Benefield?" said the hot young officer at my door, who had South Carolina blue eyes, a honeybee smile, and the cutest little dimple in his chin. His partner didn't look as friendly. Or as adorable.

"Yes, sir, Officer," I said in my very best Southern charm voice. "How can I help y'all?"

"Eva, do you mind if my partner and I come in and ask you a few questions?" Officer Handsome sounded all smooth and sweet, but I knew there had to be a stinger in there somewhere.

"Did something happen that nobody told me about?" I asked him. In situations like this, I have found that it's best to just put it out there. When information is your only power, you crave it in large quantities. We were both after the same thing, and it was a contest about who could learn the most from the other first, and get the upper hand.

"Are there firearms in this house, young lady?" Officer Suspicious asked.

"I can't talk to you until my dad gets home." I was feeling more confident about that excuse. I'd used it a couple of times by now. I was getting the hang of being evasive. Funny how that stuff happens to you, without you even having to think about it. Why doesn't it work like that in chemistry class?

"Why don't you go ahead and give him a call, then, Miss Benefield." Officer Handsome smiled and maybe even winked at me? Then he stood there, and he waited. He didn't move back from the door. He did not turn and head back to his squad car. He was just there. Holding space. Cops are good at this sort of thing.

I stepped inside and psycho-dialed my dad until he finally picked up on like the fifth try.

"Dad, the police are here," I whispered. "They are asking about guns. What do I do?"

"Tell them to go away. Tell them they can't talk to you unless I'm there; you're a minor. It will have to wait until I get home," my dad said, sounding way less alarmed than I thought he should. Had he been expecting this?

"They want to come in, Dad. They're like waiting right here on the porch."

"You're a smart girl, Eva, and I know you can handle yourself," my dad said. "But you're also a minor. You don't have to talk to them. They aren't allowed to interview you unless a parent is present, and they damn well know that. Tell them to go away. I'll be home later tonight. They can come back another time."

"Yeah, but you will be, right?" I mean, it was a little touch and go with his time commitments since he was trying to get back together with Ashley. She always found a reason to delay him at the last minute. It was impossible to predict with any precision. It was always a Tilt-A-Whirl ride in Doug and Ashley World. I got the feeling my dad spent a lot of his time stuck at the top, upside down.

"What does that mean?" my dad asked brusquely.

"I mean, will you really be home tonight? Or just you'll maybe be home tonight?"

"Yes, Eva, I'll definitely be home tonight. Tell the police they can come by tomorrow."

"So definitely tonight."

"Yes, that's what I said." And then he hung up. I was thinking, *Yeah, but you say a lot of things.* The cops went away, for the moment anyway. Officer Handsome gave me his card. I hung on to it. Well, that dimple was awfully cute. My dad showed up late that night looking like somebody who had been struck by lightning and lived. But I was so, so glad he was home.

CHAPTER 17

MERRY CHRISTMAS, MOTHERFUCKERS

Christmas was jingle belling on its merry way across the Low Country, turning the marsh grass into frigid, breakable crystals of green and white. Charleston was all lit up and rosy like a sea widow whose ship captain has just pulled back into port. All the ghosts came out at Christmas, rattling their bones up and down the cobblestones, searching the high street for long lost yuletide lovers, and terrifying the tourists for tips.

I got the text that I knew would be coming during fourth-period French. This is what it said.

And he has given us this command: Anyone who loves God must also love their brother and sister . . . John 4:20

I know this must look cryptic and indecipherable to y'all, but that's just because you haven't translated the Rosetta stone of my dad's texts at that time. Everything was always a Bible verse, like he needed God's validation to say anything at all that Ashley might see and use as ammunition against him, even though they were supposedly together again. I texted him back a question mark, but I knew what he meant just as sure as if he'd said what he meant in the first place. Here's what he texted me back.

I'd like you to come down to Florida for Xmas and meet ur baby sis.

I mean, I can't say I was surprised. I had sort of been waiting for this. I knew it was unavoidable. I wanted to meet my baby sister at some point—obviously. But to say I had mixed emotions about my dad's holiday plans would be the understatement of the century. They don't even make emojis for how I was feeling. I really did not want to see Ashley. You didn't have to be a calculus whiz to do the math and figure out who was sending the cops and CPS to our door. And I was not in a state of merry Xmas denial like my dad was. I could just envision all of us standing around some yule log, torn to bits, bleeding all over Alicia's carpet, with my dad smiling away like everything was *White Christmas*.

I had sort of been planning on spending the holiday with Pete and his family. They always did it up right over there, a real traditional Carolina Christmas, and their house was so beautiful. Plus I was head over heels for Pete. I didn't want to spend ten minutes away from him, let alone a whole holiday. And all my friends were here in Charleston. Bev and Ben were here. My brother John was talking about coming into town. I had nobody in Bradenton but my dad. And also, allow me to say this one more time for emphasis: I did NOT want to see Ashley. I was cool with the twelfth of never on that front.

Of course, I did wind up going to Florida for Christmas. Big shocker there, right? Another life-changing decision that I did not get to make for myself. My dad was pretty insistent on the subject, and I had learned to pick my battles. I stayed at my dad's condo poised at the edge of some bog north of town. Ashley brought Emerson by on Christmas Eve. Ashley was wearing a sparkly red bodycon mermaid affair, six-inch stilettos, and Wet N Wild #666 lipstick. We were going to a midnight choral service. That woman never knew how to read a room.

After church, we all had to pretend to be merry for Emerson's sake. I don't know why we bothered. Ashley was demonic. Alicia was worse. And Emerson was cranky and couldn't have cared less. It was well past her bedtime, and she was refusing to stay still for the interminable family photos in front of some horrible Boca Christmas tree. I felt a panic attack rising and excused myself to the loo. Alicia and Ashley followed me in and cornered me by the sink, whispering some shit about my dad poisoning my mom and how he was going to kill us all, too. I'm thinking, *That's just great. Merry Christmas, motherfuckers.*

I told my dad the next morning on the way back to Charleston about what the evil elves had said to me at church. I could tell that he had heard me. But it was like he didn't let it sink in. Whenever he was trying to make things work again with

Ashley, he just froze. He just couldn't metabolize the algorithm. When we got home, there was a letter from CPS in the box informing us that I had to move out of the house pending an investigation into my dad and the safety of my living situation. Then Roxy bounced without leaving a note.

I wasn't too upset about having to move out of my house. Honestly, I was a little relieved. I just couldn't relax in that house anymore anyway. There was always some black swan popping out of the drapes or pulling up in the driveway or banging on the front door. I knew that at Ben and Beverly's, at least life would be predictable and organized, maybe even a little boring, which sounded excellent to me right about then. Ben was still recovering from being wounded in Afghanistan. Things were quiet over there, and I needed some downtime, bro. Plus, I was going to be a senior next year, and I wanted to be able to focus on my schoolwork. I had to grow up and get serious at some point.

I moved a week later. After that, my dad was mostly in Bradenton. I think my dad felt like he had to make up for lost time with Emerson. But I knew firsthand that you can't make up for lost time with your kids. Once that's gone, it's gone for good. You're not going to find that time floating on the surface of the water like a lost flip-flop.

Just as I had expected, life at Ben and Bev's was soothing and predictable. And boring. I went to school and hung out with Pete. When I wasn't with Pete, we were Snapchatting. And I was starting to focus on learning how to take proper care of myself. I was eating healthy meals, going to bed at a decent hour, waking up early, and running sometimes by myself and sometimes with Pete. I didn't come home to a naked ballerina sprawled out on the kitchen counter anymore. These were all checkmarks in the plus column. Yet I still felt uncomfortable. It wasn't my home. I didn't even unpack for a month.

I don't mean to sound ungrateful. It was so nice of Ben and Bev to take me in, especially since I could tell Ben was reluctant. Honestly, I can't blame him. First of all, he was still recuperating from being shot. And second, I wasn't his kid; I shouldn't have been his problem. From practically the day I was conceived, Ben said he had known he would wind up being responsible for me one day, and now here we were, right where Ben knew we would be. I told him I was sorry, and he said I didn't have to apologize, but I felt like I did. I know he didn't mean it, but Ben had always made me feel just a little bit guilty about being born.

Things changed completely when Ben caught me smoking pot in my room, which I get was not the smoothest move I have ever made in my life. The peace was disturbed from that point on, and I honestly felt like it was an overreach. I went from being a good girl going through a rough time to a lying drug fiend who could not be trusted, like, at all or ever again. This made no sense to me. And what was frustrating was there didn't seem to be a way to win back their faith in me. My brother is a very black-and-white person, which is tough for somebody like me, who exists almost exclusively in the gray.

I knew I wasn't a bad kid. I was a good kid who messed up once. Once. Okay, maybe twice. Three times tops. I wasn't supposed to be smoking weed, I get it. I tried to work it out with them. I said I was sorry about a thousand times. I promised never to do it again. I obeyed their curfews and submitted to daily drug tests. Yes, you read that right. But okay, I did the crime, so I had to do my time. Fair was fair. But after a while, it started to feel a little like life without parole.

Part of the problem was Bev and Ben were still in their twenties. They weren't even parents of their own kids yet, let alone somebody else's teenager, who came with special handling instructions. And truthfully, Ben was right about one thing—I shouldn't have been their problem to begin with.

When I was living with my dad, even if I messed up sometimes, which all teenagers do no matter how good you are—and if you don't ever mess up, honestly, seek help—my dad would get mad at me in the moment. But he never stayed mad. He wouldn't punish me for the rest of my life because of one stupid mistake. At least not until Ashley moved in. Then things changed, but it wasn't all his fault.

I could feel Ben looking over my shoulder to see who I was texting. I just peaced out, which is what I do in response to stress. I was also coping by staying on the move. When Pete wasn't around, I was driving around town or hanging with my friend Miles. Miles was great company. I met him because he lived next door to Pete's grandparents, and I loved him because he saw the funny side of everything.

My crew was a unique Charleston blend. Roxy and Miles and I were the Wando sewer rats. Pete was at Porter-Gaud, the fancy prep school, spookily enough, on the banks of the

Ashley River, right in Charleston proper. My friend Taylor was at a Christian high school out in Greenwood, but I went and picked her up every weekend. We were all going in different directions, but we all gathered back at the hive every weekend like honeybees.

CPS finally wrapped up their investigation and, of course, cleared my dad completely. This surprised no one. That cleared the way for me to go home, but where was home at this point? I thought about it. Did I want to go back to that house? Roxy wasn't there anymore, and my dad was in Florida for the most part. Our relationship was happening over text, and I was in a weird way kinda okay with that. I decided to move back to Preservation Place, because it was my real home, and because at least there I didn't have to pee in a cup every day.

CHAPTER 18

THE WORLD WAS MY OYSTER, AND THEN I GOT SHUCKED

That final summer before my senior year at Wando was one of those times that you wished could last forever because you knew you were at the end of something important. And at the same time, you're dying for it to come to an end because you can't wait to see what comes next.

Pete's parents were out of town for most of that summer. They left for Europe at the beginning of May and then just decided to stay there. I don't remember anybody's folks being around much that summer, come to think of it. It was like the summer of no parents. We were all orphans together, standing on the edge of a cliff, ready to dive in. We went to the beach, went out on the boat fishing, got overserved Aperol spritzes at a dive joint in Shem Creek, ate oysters by the barrelful, and basically did a whole lot of nothing as we watched the sun go down on the last summer of our childhood.

I can still see us, golden boys and apricot girls, long, lazy limbs thrown over the arms of our sand chairs, basking in the gouache of late afternoon. Pete and I had the run of his whole place by the water. We'd lie out on the lawn that sprawled and tumbled like the hills of Ireland all the way down to the emerald-green sea. And there was a dock and their boats, and even a boathouse. Down the road, there was a country house, with hundreds of acres, where the boys could just tear it up and have fun.

Miss Maevie, who took care of Pete's younger brothers, was looking after the main house and cooked for us all. She had a lot to keep track of, so she didn't really bother about Pete and me too much beyond making sure we got fed and didn't run too hog wild. I think she figured we were old enough to take care of ourselves, and she was for the most part right. Close enough for South Carolina in the summertime anyway. We spent most days out on the water, or going wakeboarding or surfing or fishing the Low Country for redfish or snapper and shad roe because our friend William, who lived in Jonesville, loves that gross shit.

You can tell where a kid comes from around here by what they hunt and fish. If you're fishing for shad, there's no way you grew up anywhere close to town. We'd tease him all the time about it, but William didn't care. He fished that roe like it was the pearl in the oyster and could not understand why we didn't agree. I respected him for that. I like a man who stands for something, even if that something is shad roe. I tried really hard for Will's sake, but it was a nonstarter for me. I'm just way too suburban.

In the afternoons, we'd motor back to Pete's and barbecue in the backyard and talk about what we were all going to do now that we were seniors. Everybody was talking about applying to colleges by then. I wanted to go to the College of Charleston to study art and design. Pete was thinking about West Point but was also considering Ole Miss because of the good duck hunting down there.

Most nights, Pete and I hung out and looked at the stars and cuddled and gabbed for hours. We never ran out of stuff to say to each other, which I loved about us. We'd mostly hang in Pete's tractor shed, which was more like a renovated man cave with garage doors that opened up on to the lawn and a view of the water. It looked like this really drip club if you looked past the cinder block walls. There was even a pizza oven.

Then finally, senior year began, and while it may sound strange in light of what ultimately happened, I had the best year ever. Which in a way made things almost harder when everything fell apart. I, of course, didn't spend nearly enough time in class, despite the best of intentions. Most of the time, I was kicking it with Miles, partying on the beach with my friends, surfing, just being a kid, and spending every waking moment with Pete, my future husband and the father of my three future children and two future golden retrievers. I felt like a real live girl ready to graduate high school just like a normal person.

My dad was doing better, too. We were working out and running together when he was in town. And as it did for me, the physical activity was helping him manage his stress. He told me he was in therapy, and it seemed like it was helping. I knew money was still an issue. I had come home to another foreclosure notice on the front door, which gave the neighbors another triple scoop to dish over. So I wasn't surprised when my dad suggested that we find me an apartment close to school so we could rent out our house and use the income to pay down the mortgage. And this is when the absolute best part of my senior year started. I got my own apartment. My own apartment, by myself. Do you know what that does for the social career of a teenager? I was almost famous.

In retrospect, I realize this was not normal and probably seemed pretty sus to my friends' parents, who were, I admit, scandalized by the idea of their kids hanging out in my entirely unsupervised home. But I was responsible. And my dad stayed with me when he was in town. I had no problem with my situation. I knew how to run a house by then. I wasn't a complete savage. I have manners.

Pete would come over after school most days, sometimes even stay overnight, and it was amazing to live with no curfews, just letting our conversation flow until we fell asleep. Whenever I needed anything, my dad was always right there. If I was late for class, or felt like skipping, I'd just text him for an absence note, and he'd send it right away. He had my back. I knew I could count on him like that.

I fixed up my little apartment all cute and cozy, and it became the hangout palace for all my friends. Everybody would go to class—or not go to class, as the case might be—and then meet back at my place. It was like summer stayed around all year long. I watched the marsh grass go from green to gold to brown to white and then back to green again. And then, at last, it was time to graduate, and I have to confess, I almost didn't make it through, which really upset me because I wanted to graduate with the rest of my friends, not with the randos who had to do summer school.

Wando took pity on me and made me do a long list of chores around the school grounds to make up "seat time," by which they meant time my ass was not in my seat in class. I raked rocks. I weeded. I helped out in the cafeteria for a few weeks. The administration had chalked my absences up to the long tail of trauma, and I think they were right about that, so they got creative and let me slide. That was cool of them. They were a big school, too big to make exceptions very easily.

My dad almost didn't make it to my commencement ceremony because: Ashley. But somehow, he made it up to be with me, and there we both are in the pictures for the history books: I in a cap and gown, and my dad in dire need of a shave and a haircut. I'm standing there, grinning like an idiot with another one of those stupid sunflowers in my hand. My dad has his arm around me, smiling like there was no tomorrow, which of course there wasn't.

CHAPTER 19

LOVE AND DEATH
IN THE TIME OF COVID

In the spring of 2020, right before my nineteenth birthday, COVID hit and Charleston shut its doors, shut the bridges, shut the bars and the ferries and the wedding halls and the quaint shops, and threw anchor. All forward motion ceased abruptly. It felt like everyone everywhere curled up and went to sleep. It's eerie when a noisy working harbor like Charleston goes suddenly silent. The city streets became eerie and opaque. The ghosts walked. But down in Bradenton, where my dad was, life went on as usual. Down there, they were all like, *COVID who?* My dad was either trying to patch things up or fighting in court with Ashley, depending on the day. Same old same old. I didn't ask many questions, because the answers never made sense and did not have the ring of authenticity anyway.

I was in my very first semester of art school at the College of Charleston, and then all my classes went virtual, which is kind of a buzzkill when you're an art student and you need to put your hands on things in order to learn. My dad was wor-ried about me being all by myself up here and said we needed to think about letting the apartment go. He suggested I think about finding a college closer to him in Florida. I was like, *Oh hell no, dude. That dog definitely will not hunt.*

This is when we all decided I'd move in with Pete's family. I had to admit, it was lonely being stuck in my high school party pad all by myself. Pete's family was kind enough to offer, and my dad signed off, so for the whole pandemic, I lived with the Naughtons at their place on the water. This was incredibly gen-erous of them, and it was such a nice place to be, and of course Pete was there, which didn't suck. But once again, I never quite felt at home. I missed my little apartment by the Wando River, and I missed my independence.

I'm incredibly grateful to the Naughtons, but I have to admit it felt a little weird living with my boyfriend's family. I think it might have been a little uncomfortable for Pete, too, although he never said so. I think it kind of rushed our rela-tionship in a way. And for another thing, I had never lived with a big family before. I was essentially an only child growing up, and then I lost my mom, and now my dad was in Florida, and I had been taking care of myself for almost two full years. I had become something of a lone wolf. I was morphing into my future shape as the solitary salt witch of Charleston, pacing the ramparts by day, and frightening the local children.

Moving in with an intact, nice, normal, unfractured fam-ily didn't come naturally to me anymore. Also, they weren't my family—they were Pete's family. I mean, Pete and I weren't married yet, so you see what I mean about condensing our emotional timeline. As welcoming as they were, I never felt like I fit in. I wasn't comfortable, not the way I used to be when my mom was alive. You don't even notice that comfortable feeling when you have it, but when it's gone, you really miss it a lot.

Pete wasn't super supportive about helping me blend in at the beginning with his family either. The main house was quite a palace, and it was easy to get lost in all the doors and hallways and staircases. It was an old, sprawling building. Pete said it had once been a hospital for soldiers fighting in the Civil War and that there were ghosts of slaves in Confederate uniforms that walked the downstairs corridors at night, right close to where my bedroom was. I thought he made that stuff up until one day, when I was by myself downstairs, I saw the ghost. I called Pete at work, and I was like, "Pete, the ghost is in the hallway. I can see him. What do I do?"

"Don't worry," Pete said calmly. "He does that all the time. Just let him walk. You'll be fine. Don't get in his way, though."

"What will happen if I do?" I whispered.

"Well, I don't know," Pete said. "But it's probably best not to find out."

Pete left a lot up to faith that way. I guess you can be that way when nothing has ever gone wrong in your whole life. I found out later this was actually not true. Pete had faced some hard times, right inside his own picture-perfect family, that I never even knew about. Everyone has secrets. Everybody is haunted by something. It's just that Pete didn't get upset or feel the need to talk about it. He was happy to just let the ghosts walk and stay out of their way.

I was out on the beach almost every day, and then once it warmed up and the bridges reopened, I was back on Sullivan's, planted in the sand on 22½, just kind of staring out to sea like in *The French Lieutenant's Woman*. I felt a change rising with the tide. So I waited. I watched. And then I met some girlies hanging out on the sandbar in early June, and they told me they were looking for a place in town and needed a third roommate. I was like, *You know what? Sweet. Count me in.* I didn't even talk to Pete about it first. I was beginning to develop a real appetite for disruption.

The sandbar girlies and I found a cute little duplex on Strawberry Lane. For real, Strawberry Lane, how cute is that? And it was right in downtown Charleston. I sent my dad pics, and he was like, "Looks great, Eva," and he sent me money for the deposit. Even Pete was cool with it. So my two new roomies and I moved into the top-floor unit, and everything was peaches for about five minutes, until I figured out my new girlies were massive party hounds. That was not going to work out.

Listen, I'm not a freak. I like to have fun like everybody else. But every night, there was a full-on rager at my place, and I was over it toot sweet. I had enough confusion in my life. I had faced actual chaos. I didn't need a self-created teenage wasteland in my living room on the daily. I wanted a little peace and quiet. Somewhere along the line, I had grown up. And with my mom dying, and then after everything with my dad and Ashley, I had managed to mature a lot more quickly than most kids my age. Which made it tough to find compatible roommates.

Pete sailed to Bermuda with his friend Nathan that summer. Pete had decided to go to school at the Citadel, which meant he had to live on campus during the school year. So that summer, he had some steam built up. Nathan's dad was a movie star, so that kid had a really nice clipper. They were going to be gone for a whole month, and they couldn't take their phones for reasons that made no kind of sense to me. I expected to feel pretty lost without Pete. And I did miss him a lot. But I refused to be that girl. So I started focusing on myself. I surfed, I ate healthy, I was painting. I had a part-time job at this stupid restaurant, saving up money to get the hell out of my apartment and find my own place. I was hanging out a ton with Miles, who was someone I knew I could rely on to be there for me, no matter what did or did not happen.

I started looking for a new job, because I hated the one I had at the chicken-and-waffle house. I made like almost no dollars. I had a side hack on the DL shuttling folks to the bars on Sullivan's at night while the island was still shut down because of COVID. Some of the bar owners set up a deal with the kids who had boats, and we'd motor people around the back of the island. It paid a hundred bucks a head, so you could make pretty good cheddar every night shuttling bootleg drunks back and forth who may or may not have been contagious. But even though everybody told me it was perfectly legit, it felt sus to me. I'm way too anxious to be an outlaw.

Then one day, finally, the universe blinked. While I was

having coffee at the Brown Fox, the coffee shop in the Old Village that had been my home away from home since middle school, I noticed a sign in the window that said, "We're hiring." I was like, *Oh my God, that's my job right there in the window.* I talked to Biz, the owner, who I've known since I was like seven, and I was like, "Biz, you have to hire me." I'd been foaming milk there for nothing for like centuries. Biz was like, "Yeah, sure, Eva. Put in an application," and I did, and like two days later, I was hired and scheduled for onboarding.

I was the most excited I'd been in a while. I know, it was only a dead-end job. But all my first times had happened at the Brown Fox—first date, first kiss, first macchiato. Plus, as you may have noticed, I love coffee. I love everything about coffee—coffee people, coffeehouses, coffee cake, coffee talk, coffee tables. I could go on, but I'll spare you. Even my dad owned a coffee shop before I was born. It was in my DNA.

My plan was to work at the Brown Fox for a while, save up my money, focus on my artwork, get my own little artist's shack in the Low Country, on the water, where I could paint, and draw, and stare out over the water, and hang out with Pete once he got home from the sea. And best of all, I'd never have to come home to the beer pong twins again. I was supposed to start training at the Brown Fox the morning of September 28, so the night before, I went out with my friends for one last booya before I started foaming milk full-time and all my friends went off to college.

My dad was down in Florida, supposedly living his happy

home life with Ashley. I could tell things weren't going great, but my dad didn't tell me about it, because I had asked him not to. But I could read between the lines that there was a lot of *she loves me, she loves me not* going on down there. I would ask him, but I knew I wasn't getting a straight answer. He was a true believer, 100 percent invested in the dream, even though it was really a never-ending nightmare.

About a week before, my dad had called to tell me they were all moving to Maryland for some reason I didn't understand. I was like, "Okay, cool, Dad." I wasn't that invested. I knew Ashley was from there and Alicia had just inherited her mother's house, so whatever. It did cross my mind that Ashley might be looking for a fresh jurisdiction to torture my dad in since she was about out of options in Manatee County, but it wasn't my business anymore. I had aged out of CPS visits. She couldn't touch me. And I genuinely hoped they'd be happy together, for my dad's sake. But I doubted it. It's weird to be a teenager and have a better understanding of your parent than they have of themselves. It felt unnatural.

My dad was back and forth all that week, picking up stuff from storage in Charleston and rushing back eight hours nonstop to be in Florida to help Ashley pack up a clamshell. The plan was for my dad to rent the truck, pack the truck, drive the truck, and tow the car, while Ashley, Alicia, Emerson, and Ashley's two cats went on ahead. Sounds about right. My dad did everything. Paid for everything. Ashley and Alicia got their tips done and complained about the heat.

I called my dad the night before the big move just to check in on him. Looking back, I think I was worried even then, because I got nervous when he didn't pick up, which was unusual for me. I normally would blow that off. But then I thought about it. *Whatever. He's in his bubble down there getting ready to move.* That part was all true. *He'll be fine*, I thought. That part wasn't.

That day, September 27, 2020, a bunch of us had gone surfing in some truly sorrowful swell. No shredders in sight. Still waters. We were all just hanging around waiting for 5:00, when our friend's shift behind the bar at Shem's started, and we could order cocktails without getting carded. For some reason, I felt really sick to my stomach. Like the panic you feel two hours after eating a bad oyster, when the ptomaine poisoning starts to set in, and you realize what you're in for and that there's nothing you can do about it now.

I had to sit down and put my head between my knees because I thought I was going to faint. I called Bev and told her I didn't feel good. I was afraid I had COVID, or monkey pox, or stomach cancer. I'm always convinced I have a rare and terminal disease that will sneak up on me. To this day, I get one little twinge and I think I'm gonna drop dead right there on the sand. Only I never do. This fact should reassure me. But it doesn't.

"Eva, you're fine," Bev said. She was obviously by now used to this sort of thing with me. "You're probably just tired or hungry or something. Did you have your coffee yet today?" Why is it that whenever I don't feel well, the people in my family are always like, *Yep, Eva must be having caffeine withdrawal again.* Like I ran on the stuff or something. Then again . . . not far off.

"Yes, I just killed my second cold brew," I said, still convinced that my prognosis was probably poor.

"Just take a few deep breaths, sugar, and if you feel better, then drive on over here and spend the night. That way, you won't have to hit traffic on the way to your first day of work tomorrow. But if you don't feel better, Eva, go get a COVID test before you come out here." Honestly, I felt better just hearing Bev's voice. I calmed down instantly whenever I talked to her. She was like the Eva whisperer.

"Okay, I'll come over. I already feel better just talking to you. I don't know what's wrong with me. You're right. Probably hunger. Thanks so much, Bev, for, like, everything." She laughed and blew me a kiss through the phone, and I started to hang up. Then the dread hit my stomach again, and I remembered what I had wanted to ask her. "Oh, hey, Bev? I've been trying to get hold of my dad. Did he check in with you guys, by any chance? I've been calling him, but he's not picking up. They're leaving for Maryland in the morning."

"No, haven't heard from him. All right, see you in a little while, cutie," Bev said, intentionally ignoring that stuff about my dad and rushing me off the phone. I don't even know why I asked. My dad and Ben weren't in touch. Not really since my mom died, and definitely not since Ashley moved in. Nobody wanted to go near the subject of my dad and the girl from *The Ring.* My family was afraid to even mention her, for fear that Ashley would come slithering out of the TV and end the world.

Bev said she'd feed me when I got there. Just the mention of food made me want to throw up. I thought, *Maybe I should get a COVID test*, and then I was like, *No. It's nerves.*

I called my dad again, but he didn't pick up. I saw a text from him that came through around 4:30 that said, "How r u doin pumpkin?" He only called me *pumpkin* when he was in a good mood, so that relieved me. I thought, *Maybe Bev's right. I'm just hungry.* I drove over to Mount Pleasant and sat down at Bev's table, but I could only pick at my dinner. Then I didn't so much fall asleep as lose consciousness on the couch. I didn't wake up until the next morning, drenched in a cold sweat. I had no idea how I had gotten into the bed.

I looked at my phone first thing to see if I'd heard from my dad. He always texted me by 6:00 a.m. at the latest. He was a morning person, like me. But there was no morning Bible verse from him. No cute pictures of Emerson. He hadn't responded to any of my texts since yesterday. This triggered me. It brought back memories of my mom when she didn't text me back. This was about the time the alarm bells started shrieking in my head.

I called my dad again and then started psycho-texting him. I even considered texting Ashley to see if everything was all right, but I immediately thought better of that idea. I kept staring at the last words he sent to me the day before. He had called me *pumpkin*. Everything had to have been fine. I stared at his text so long the letters started to pull apart, float around, and lose their meaning. I felt dizzy and strange. Like I was starting to separate from my body. I texted my dad one more time and then jumped into the shower. If I was going to face disaster, I at least wanted to do it with clean hair and a cute fit. Fashion is armor.

As soon as I got out of the shower, I checked to see if I'd heard from him, but still nothing. I wondered if our phones had been shut off. Hey, it happened sometimes. He would blame it on the towers, and I let him, although I guessed most times he hadn't paid the bill. *Maybe he's fighting with Ashley and can't respond.* That tracked. I went to dial him and then I thought, *No, if they're fighting, that'll probably really piss her off.* Then I was like, *Whatever. Good. They deserve it.* And I called him again.

These are the thoughts I distracted myself with, so I didn't go down a rabbit hole and start imagining the worst. In the meantime, I had to get ready for my first day at my new job. I tried to proceed normally. I pulled on my favorite comfy tee, tied my orange Converse, did a quick fit check, and then texted and called my dad a bunch more times, just to really put it to Ashley. The last time I dialed, the call dropped. Maybe a tower really was down.

I did a quick search for outages, and I thought I found a notification of an outage due to a tower being struck by lightning. *See?* I thought. *You're being ridiculous over nothing. It's been AT&T all along. But what if it isn't? What if he's been in a car wreck?* I searched "Charleston man gets into an accident in Bradenton, Florida." Nothing. *Should I call the hospitals?* I didn't even know what hospitals were down there. I was starting to get frantic, reaching out in every crazy direction I could think of, hoping to grab on to a branch. But I came up empty-handed. There was just a gray, verse-less void where my dad used to be.

I still have the texts that I sent to my dad that day. I look at them sometimes. It's me telling my dad over and over that I'm freaking out and he needs to call me right away because I have anxiety disorder and am on the verge of a major panic attack. I can see the rolling waves of fear roaring toward shore in my text bubbles. I had numbed out to my dad's comings and goings for so long, and then suddenly, all the feelings I had been blocking for months burst through the fortifications, and I was nose deep in the big muddy.

By the time my uncle called me at work about 11:00 that same morning, I knew what had happened to my dad. "Eva," he said, his voice sounding all shaky and thick as sludge, "I have some really bad news to tell you."

"He's dead, right?" I said flatly. "She killed him, didn't she? That's what happened? She shot him?"

"Yes, I'm so sorry, honey. Your dad died last night. But how did you know that, Eva?"

But it was not hard to know how things would turn out. It was only hard to say when. Still, even though it was completely predictable, almost inevitable, when the shit finally goes down, it's still a terrible shock.

My Uncle Dave sounded sadder than I had ever heard him. My dad's cousin Tommie was on the phone, too. He and my dad had flown together in the navy, so they were very close. Almost like brothers.

"She's claiming your dad attacked her and that she shot him in self-defense. Of course, we know that's not true," said Uncle Dave, who is a pastor.

"We'll get to the bottom of this, don't you worry," said Tommie.

"I'm so sorry, darlin'," said Uncle Dave. "I'm gonna fly up there just as soon as I can get a flight. I'll be there soon, sweetheart."

"Is she in jail?" I wanted her in jail.

"No, they haven't arrested her yet," Tommie said. "They're investigating, but I told them there wasn't any way Doug would have hurt Ashley. No way. He bent over backward for that woman."

"The police said your dad was unarmed," Dave said.

"Emerson?" I asked, realizing I now had a little sister I might never get the chance to know.

"Emerson is fine. Alicia and the baby had gone for a walk to the splash park when it happened," Uncle Dave said.

"Don't worry, honey," Tommie told me. "The police are investigating. Now we have to trust the authorities and be patient. They'll find out who's responsible for this. Is there anything you need right away until we can get there?" I knew there were probably a lot of things I needed right away, but right off the top of my head, I couldn't come up with a single thing. Thank God the men in my family kind of took over at that point, because I was useless.

"I don't know. I think I have to go." I felt like I was going to faint.

"Okay, Eva, we'll call you as soon as we get into town, and we'll let you know if we hear anything further from the police," Dave said. "The police may contact you, so don't be alarmed if you get a call from Manatee County. I'm calling the lawyer to find out next steps."

As soon as I hung up, I felt the fight-or-flight chemicals surging through my body. I grabbed my keys, hopped in the whip, and took off. I didn't even know where I was going. Pete was at school. I wound up at Matt's house. He still lived down the street from my old house on Preservation Place. A few of my friends were hanging out there, too—Miles and Trent, Taylor and Sadie. I just sat down on the stoop without saying anything, kind of staring into space.

"Eva, what's wrong with you?" Miles asked. I must have looked like I had just been hit by a truck.

"My dad's dead," I said. "Ashley shot him."

Everybody looked at me, stunned speechless.

"Holy shit, Eva. What are we going to do with you?" Matt said finally.

"I don't know," I said. "I guess I have no parents now."

"What the fuck?" said Miles. Taylor came and practically sat on top of me and put her arms around me. The weight of her body anchored me to the earth; otherwise, I felt like I might just float away. I only knew I was still alive because I could feel the weight of her bending my shoulder the wrong way. I could hear my phone blowing up in my pocket. It was Pete, who was in class at the Citadel. I texted him that my dad had been in an accident. I didn't want to tell Pete the truth until I could see him in person.

"Let's do something fun," Matt said, like I might fly into a million pieces if he didn't take charge and get us all into motion. "What do you want to do, Eva? Come on. Think of something fun. You're always good at that."

"Let's go get drunk and enjoy this last peaceful night before all of this becomes real," I said. "Because you know once all this shakes out, it's going to get crazy, and I really don't want to think about that right now." We all knew where we were going. We didn't even have to say it. We all just got up as if on cue and headed for Shem's.

Miles had to rent the room because he was the only one who was over twenty-one. I remember our room number was 111, which was my mother's favorite number. She always said 111 was the number of angels. I remember thinking that she was sending me a sign that my dad had made it safely into heaven. Now they were together again, and he was safe. He was back in my mom's arms, where Ashley couldn't hurt him anymore.

We dumped our stuff in the room and then went and sat on the dock. I ordered multiple Aperol spritzes and watched the shrimp boats dock with their haul, spraying down their pole nets before harboring over for the night. In the dying light of that last day of Indian summer, and as the first brushstrokes of fall began to sweep the low land, I watched an egret skimming across the golden marsh grass in search of supper. She felt her way as if by instinct along the spidery tributaries that rush from the fall line toward Charleston Bay before dumping into the intracoastal waterway and disappearing into the gray-green sea.

"I guess this means I'm an orphan now," I said to Miles, who was swaying on the end of the dock, half-heartedly skipping stones in between sips of his dark and stormy.

"Yeah," Miles said, shooting me a whiskey wink. "Who isn't?"

CHAPTER 20

BETWEEN THE DEVIL
AND THE DEEP BLUE SEA

We cremated my dad a few days later, when the medical examiner released his body after making a finding of homicide. Ashley's kill shot had caught him in the side and ripped through both of his lungs. He lived long enough to make it to the hospital, but ultimately he had drowned in his own blood. My whole family from Texas, Dave and his wife, Roxy, my cousins, Tommie and his family, and my dad's other brother, Wes, all gathered to scatter my dad's ashes on Sullivan's Island Beach. It was a small group in the end, for my dad. I watched the offshore breeze swirl him around and up and out to open sea. For a navy pilot, it seemed like the right place for him.

Afterward, we all headed over to Dunleavy's Pub, where my parents had met. We sat outside and ate piles of wings and fried oysters. My dad would have liked that. No fuss. Just good food and family, under a powder-blue South Carolina sky. I felt sad that my mom and dad did not get the full lives they were en-titled to. My dad got himself caught up between the devil and the deep blue sea, and that day on Sullivan's, the sea won. Now I wanted the devil arrested.

A couple of days later, the family went home, back to their calm, everyday worlds where people did not get killed by their spouses. Everybody's lives went back to normal . . . everybody's except for mine. I wondered if Emerson would remember my dad. She will only know my dad through the stories Ashley and Alicia will tell her. She might never know who her dad was. That he loved her very much. That he died fighting for her.

When my grandfather passed away, my dad and his broth-ers banded together, locked arms, and got through the storm. If I'd had a sibling closer to my age, if Emerson had been older, maybe we would have done that, too. We'd have pulled to-gether and become tight. When my mom died, I had my dad to lean on, and he was really great about being my rock—for a while anyway. My dad was the only one who really got me. He listened. He was patient. He waited while I struggled to spit out whatever it was I had to say. He knew I had trouble expressing myself. He knew how to coax me out of my shell. My dad always knew how to make things better for me. Now he was gone. Now I had to learn how to make things better for myself.

In the days and weeks after his death, I have to confess I wasn't too good at taking care of myself. The shock and violence was too much for me. Plus, the press was all over the place. First it was the local affiliates, and then the networks started calling. I started seeing THE BLACK SWAN MURDER TRIAL in the tabloids for the first time. Everybody was like, *Oh my God, Eva. We're so sorry for your loss. Are you okay?* And I was all, *Yeah, I'm okay.* And I *was* okay, and that freaked everybody out—myself included. *Shouldn't I be falling apart or something? Shouldn't I be beside myself with grief? Am I dead inside? Will I ever feel anything ever again?*

I circled the rim for a while, I'm not gonna lie. I was erratic. Making rash and often ill-informed decisions. My Uncle Dave and my brothers were checking on me in the beginning, but that trailed off. What were they gonna do? They had families and lives of their own. Ben and Bev had a new baby on the way. Pete was the best, though, just there for me, being his strong and quiet self. I didn't need him to say anything. And I didn't have to say anything. It was just nice being quiet with somebody who knew how I felt. We didn't need words. I had a lot to figure out, and quickly. I had fifteen bucks in the bank, and rent was due in like the next five minutes. Somebody suggested starting a GoFundMe account for me, but I said no. I didn't want to owe any favors to anybody or depend on anybody ever again.

My dad's lawyer in Florida, Stephanie, called a month after my dad died to tell me that Ashley had finally been arrested. "Took them long enough" was all I said. I wouldn't wish harm on anyone, but it did feel good that something bad had finally happened to the right person instead of the wrong one. When you're a victim of a violent crime like I was, like my dad was, you really get a feeling for the weight and the wait of justice.

Accountability feels super slow. Ashley spent exactly seventeen days in jail before she was released on a $100,000 surety bond with an ankle bracelet and a curfew. She moved in with Alicia and Emerson, so she basically got her way. It felt like Manatee County had grounded Ashley for killing my father.

I had started my job at the Brown Fox. Biz, the owner, held my job for me, which was so sweet of her. And I wanted to get back to work. I mean, what else was I supposed to do? It felt better to be busy, and I needed the money. I love Biz, and I respect her so much. She taught me a lot of what I know and use with my company Ghost Cowboy today, about creating a community-built brand. I think some people thought it was weird I went back to work so soon, but I couldn't just stand there, looking backward. I wasn't Lot's daughter. I hadn't turned into a pillar of salt. I had bills to pay.

My dad didn't have any life insurance. Lots of people ask me that, and the answer is no, not a cent on that front. Or any front. My parents thought that only one of them needed to have life insurance, and they figured my dad would die before my mom, because guys are idiots and women are the survivors. So they only covered my dad, and then my mom died and my dad was like, *Fuck!* So, after my mom's death, he raised his insurance to something like a million dollars, so I would be covered in case something happened to him. But then my dad spent all his money on that ballet and had stopped paying the premiums. It had lapsed three months before he died, and even if it hadn't, the money would have probably gone to his widow, a.k.a. Satan. I can never catch a break.

I guess it might be a good thing that I didn't really understand my financial circumstances with any clarity at the time. When I heard that my dad had been shot, my first thought was *Oh my God, I'm an orphan.* My second thought was *Oh, fuck, I'm broke, and rent is due next week, and I have literally nine bucks to my name.* Well, fifteen once Miles paid me back for gas. I called my Uncle Dave and told him I had no money. Then one of my dad's friends wired me five thousand dollars to get me through, which was so incredibly sweet of him. I knew that I'd better make the five grand last as long as I possibly could, which wasn't very long at all in an atmospheric and rapidly gentrifying tourist destination like Charleston. No ifs, ands, or buts about it. I had to hit the ground running. And it was hard. It's still hard.

Nobody wanted to talk to me about my dad, or the murder trial, or any of what had happened in my actual world, except for the media, who was always on the hunt for a hot tip. I did a little segment with *Access Hollywood*, I think, and also *Vanity Fair*. But after I started seeing the coverage, I just shut down. I turned to my TikTok community, which I had been building since before my dad died. Those were folks who knew me before I was a tabloid title. But then I totally killed my category by telling the story about my dad's death in #storytime. Suddenly, nobody wanted to hear about anything else, and I had only myself to blame. I basically dug my own grave and then lay down in it. I was now the CEO of OrphanTok.

IRL, though, people got quiet when I brought up my dad. Even my brothers. Especially my brothers. This left me with the feeling that I should just shut up about my problems. Like I was annoying people, but it wasn't actually me they were annoyed at. My dad had really tried people's patience, and he never did come to his senses in the end. I think people felt a little bit like *Well, you play with fire like Ashley, is it any wonder your house burns down?* And because of that stupid ballet, my dad had become something of what we call down here a *tribulation*. That's like a couple of steps past annoyance, and just short of *Bitch, where's my money?*

I could tell people were whispering even after he was gone. Even though I'm not the one who disappointed everybody, I felt like I was being expected to pay a debt that wasn't mine to begin with. I wonder if that's why Charleston has so many ghosts—century after century of lost souls feeling obliged to pay the price for the sins of their miscreant fathers, and then haunting the tourists when their lives didn't turn out as they'd hoped. I did not intend to be the ghost of my father's bad judgment. Or his bad debt.

I sometimes think that it's all these little things stacked up—the left-behind garbage of life; the unsaid, the undone, the unpaid, the unresolved, these are the things that haunt the living after we're gone. The ghosts in wedding gowns hovering in the trees around here are just lore for the tourists.

My dad had become a widow and orphan on the page of my life. That was his story. But it wasn't going to be my story. I wasn't going to join the legions of restless, pointless spirits haunting the Low Country. I was never going to become something that goes bump in the night; I refused to be defined by the errant ectoplasm of my fucked-up past. I had my own story to write. I had a future. I wanted to live.

I got this big, bold-ass tattoo on my arm in thick black print. It says, *October 2, 1961*, which was my dad's birthday. I thought it was better to remember his birthday, instead of his death date. Most folks don't ask me about it, but I was at brunch with Taylor, and we were a little mimosa drunk. There was a table of old people next to us. There were two men and a woman, and just as we were leaving, one of the guys at the table said, "Excuse me, but what's October 2, 1961? Wait, let me guess. Is that your dad's birthday?"

I was stunned. I didn't know what to say. I was like, "Um, yeah," because it caught me totally off guard, and also, see above re: mimosas.

"Oh, that's so sweet," the woman said. "He must have been so happy when he saw it. How did he react? Was he so happy and proud?"

"Yeah, he rolled over in his grave," I said before I could claw the words back. They just stopped dead in their tracks and looked at me, and it was so historically awkward. I mean, I should not have slapped them in the face with cold reality like that, not at brunch on a sunny Sunday in Charleston. I still think about that, and I am so embarrassed. It was rude. Folks are nice to folks down here—I mean, unless you're a tourist, and then all bets are off. It's also fucked up because my dad doesn't have a grave. My dad should have a grave. What the fuck, Eva?

CHAPTER 21

THE BULLSHIT REMAINS

My brother Ben was the executor of my father's will, which struck me as odd, because Ben wasn't my dad's son and was pretty irritated by my dad, generally speaking. Ben was already grown when my mom and dad got married, and he and my dad never really bonded on that deep of a level. It made sense that it was Ben, though, when I realized the will was written while my mom was alive. In the will, my dad's spouse got half of his estate, and we kids got the other half. The only other difference between then and now was that his wife wasn't my mom anymore; it was Ashley. My dad had left half his money to his shooter. This kind of a thing happens more often than you'd realize. It's not even unique.

Not that there was anything much to inherit besides his truck and his unpaid bills and a house that was underwater. The bank accounts were wiped. He'd spent every last cent on Ashley and that ridiculous ballet. There was no college fund, no nest egg, no life insurance, no trust fund, no nothing that could help me out. He did have some stock that wasn't worth anything yet, but my dad had told me it would be worth millions one day. The sun was always coming out tomorrow in my dad's world. He never lost hope.

Ben didn't seem so happy about being the executor, to say the least. He had to have agreed to it at some point, or then again, maybe not. My mom might have just signed him up without checking with him first. He was the eldest son. Either Ben didn't know how to handle things or just resented the intrusion, but it didn't feel like he wanted to be bothered with the state of my affairs. He didn't say much to me about the business end of the situation, and I didn't ask, but I guess I should have. But none of my other relatives were paying much attention, so I figured, why should I? Which of course is kind of ridiculous, because the fact that nobody else was paying attention was the reason I should have been following up on things. But I just couldn't, probably for the same reason nobody else could either. We all just wanted to forget about what had happened. It was easier to just let it all slide.

So I had lots of folks to blame, including myself, when, a couple of months later, as I was getting ready for work, a process server showed up on my doorstep. Surprise! For a second, I was like, *Oh my God, what has Ashley done now?* I showed Ben the papers, though, and he told me they were a notice of a lawsuit. The bank was suing me because the house was underwater. Of course they were.

Getting served with a lawsuit is scary for anybody at any time, especially if it's never happened to you before. For me, a formerly feckless, now newly minted nineteen-year-old orphan with about ten bucks to my name, it was paralyzing. I threw the legal papers in a drawer where I knew I would definitely forget all about them, grabbed my mat, and headed off to yoga. I love yoga. Coffee and yoga have been very reliable friends to me; really the best of friends, second only to Sully, who was now living with me in my ratched party pad with the beach blowout twins. I wasn't going anywhere without any of them, from here on out.

I knew that no matter what went on, I could always go to yoga and breathe for forty-five minutes, and I'd feel better, almost happy, in a way that I didn't feel guilty about. Yoga was the one place where I felt totally in control, which is funny, because yoga is supposed to be about surrender.

I must have looked pretty checked out because Mame, my yoga teacher, said she wanted to talk to me after class. Mame had been my dad's high school sweetheart, so I think she felt like she should help keep an eye on me, and she really did, actually still does, which is kind of her. Mame always knew when something was wrong and usually knew just how to make things better. She knew how to take me by the shoulders, slow me down, and remind me to breathe, which I always forget to do when I'm anxious. And breathing is kind of a good thing not to forget about.

"Eva? Are you all right? How is everything going?" Mame asked me, taking my mat out of my hands and rolling it up for me. That's when I burst into tears and told her I was being sued by the bank because the house was being foreclosed on, and now my dad was dead and they wanted $500,000 from somebody who was broke and working for minimum wage. My normally chill and always-rises-above-whatever yoga teacher grabbed me by the hand and dragged me into her office, looking super pissed, and I really hoped it wasn't at me.

"What's your brother's number?" she said, pointing to a chair for me to sit down and handing me a box of Kleenex. "I'm calling him."

"Don't call him," I said. "He can't do anything. He already told me that. Besides, he hated my dad."

"Well then, he shouldn't have agreed to be the executor," Mame said.

"I'm not sure he did agree to that," I said. But Mame was already dialing. For a yoga instructor, she moved awfully quick and with a great deal of force.

"Didn't your father have a brother—what's-his-name, Dave? Wasn't he a pastor or something? What's his number?" I showed her my phone, and before I could say *hold on a minute*, she was into my contacts and had Ben and my Uncle Dave patched in on a conference call. I was embarrassed. I didn't like to cause a fuss, but I have to admit it felt good to have somebody sticking up for me for a change. I had been drowning for weeks, and everybody just thought, *Oh, look, there's Eva waving hello from the middle of the deep blue ocean.* And then they'd wave back and move along down the beach. Thank God for high school sweethearts.

Once Mame had everybody cyber-chained in a room together, she proceeded to ask my immediate male family members all about just what the hell they had not been doing for me. She said we all need to support me now, because I was only a kid and Doug had left things in a complete mess, and how was I supposed to understand these kinds of grown-up financial matters anyway? And now I was getting sued, which was obviously traumatic at a time when I was already traumatized.

My uncle heard her, sprang into action, and told my brother to sign over the executorship to him so he could administer the estate, including some alleged safe that had supposedly gone missing. I never did find out what happened to that. A key to some lock on a treasure chest buried at the bottom of the sea that's probably empty anyway, if it ever even existed. The only thing of my dad's I'd managed to dig up so far was more debt.

Tommie had been paying $400 a month to store my dad's stuff, and the estate needed to start paying those bills, because he couldn't afford to pay it out of his own pocket anymore. At this point, I burst into tears. What? Now I had to pay for storage? But my Uncle Dave said not to worry and told Tommie he'd pick up the legal bill and the storage, and we'd get the house ready to be sold.

My Uncle Dave, and Tommie and Mame, and Ben and Bev—really all the adults that pulled together for me at that time—were such a huge help. It meant more to me than they will ever know. Because there really was a ton of stuff that needed to be done, and I didn't have the first idea how to do any of it. It was a difficult age to lose your parents. It's not like you're ten years old and everybody jumps in and takes over because you're a poor little orphan. But you're not really an adult either, even though you are legally. When you've reached the age of majority, it's easier for people to steer clear. You're your own problem now.

You know how in movies, when people have terminal cancer or something, and it's curtains for sure—you're like a dead man walking—that's when people always say, *Well, go home now and put your affairs in order?* Well, I never really knew why they always said that or what it meant until my dad died, and he had not done that. My dad had not put his affairs in order. My dad's affairs were left in complete chaos and across multiple states. And new loose ends turned up every day. Here are just some of the things the people who are left behind have to deal with when somebody gets killed and didn't have the chance to prepare for death.

THE BULLSHIT THAT REMAINS

- People who are killed still rack up fees.

- People who are killed still have pets.

- People who are killed still have mortgages and/or leases.

- People who are killed don't usually have a prepurchased funeral package or a plot.

- People who are killed have a lot of stuff that you can't throw out but still have no use for. And storage is expensive.

• People who are killed don't have time to move the weird stuff that family members should never see out of their sock drawer or off their phone.

• People who are killed don't get to express their dying wishes, so you have to guess.

• People who are killed sometimes leave their money to their killer.

I'll get back to you when I manage to tackle this list. It's currently in my junk drawer, next to the court summons from the bank.

CHAPTER 22

WHEN FROGS FLY

There's a fairy tale down here that the fishermen at the docks used to tell me when I was little. It was about a heron and a frog, and I always remembered it because I love white herons. They are my favorite waterbird—much more elegant than swans, really—and my mom told me they're the messengers of God. They do look like some kind of good omen or something swooping down like a revelation from heaven. And I also like white herons because they don't travel in a flock. They fly solo. And they do not mate for life.

Herons stand for lots of cool things—like independence, patience, serenity, and solitude, all stuff I'm trying to cultivate in my own life. Herons can be very still, so still they almost seem like statues. They can wait all day long for just the right fish to appear, without getting bored or distracted or irritated about how long it's taking. They are patience on a monument. But then, when that perfect fish comes along, they strike so fast you don't even believe you've seen it. Herons are very efficient and successful hunters, and they rarely go hungry for long.

As the story goes, one day, a heron is flying over the marsh, surveying the tide pools for dinner, when she spies a frog hopping happily along through the sweetgrass, probably on his way home to have a quiet dinner with his frog family.

Oh, that poor bird, the heron thinks, *someone must have stolen his wings. I'll give him a lift until he can find the culprit and get his own wings back.* So, the heron picks up the frog in her feet and soars way up into the sky, taking the frog higher than he's ever been in his life.

At first, the frog is like, *YOLO*, and takes in the elation of flight. He feels transformed. He looks down at the tops of the trees and marvels that the grass could grow so high. He had never seen the top of anything before. He had never imagined that there was this whole big and amazing world far above the marsh that was so much bigger than he was, and so beautiful.

But then, it starts to dawn on the poor guy that he's being carried into the sky by a strange frog who has somehow grown wings. What kind of a frog can do that? And where was this flying frog taking him? What were her intentions? Had he been seized by a predator? Was she going to eat him? Or let him tumble back into the weeds, never to be heard from again? Would he ever have dinner with his frog family again?

So now, the frog gets freaked out AF. He no longer feels the joy of flight or sees the beauty of the world above the marsh. He's miserable up there in the clouds, far away from his friends and family down below, who are hopping happily through the Low Country without a care in the world. He tries to cry out to them, but they are too far away, and they can't hear him. So, naturally, the frog is triggered. He feels the beginnings of a panic attack and begs the heron to let him go home.

"Please put me back where you found me," the terrified frog says. "I'm scared and lonely, and I'm about ready to have a panic attack. I have an anxiety disorder, and I want to go home."

So the heron is like, *If that's what you want, I'll put you back where I found you.* And the heron swoops down from the heavens and sets the frog back down in the marsh grass. Then she soars back up into the sky and disappears.

At first, the frog is so relieved and overjoyed to be back home where he belongs. He hops home and tells his frog family, and then they all sit down and have dinner to celebrate his safe return. But then, once the thrill of rescue and reunion is over, he starts to think back on what it was like to have wings and soar through the sky, looking down on the world instead of always looking up at things. He suddenly wishes that he had wings or that he hadn't begged the heron to put him back down on the earth quite so soon. Maybe he should have asked her to come and visit him again and take him for another ride high into the sky.

The frog tries to tell his friends about the giant world that he has seen beyond the marsh, but they either don't believe him or think he's nuts and avoid him. He's a freak now, and when the other frogs see him coming, they hop the other way. Even his family is embarrassed. Nobody understands the frog any-more. And who can blame them? The frog doesn't even under-stand himself. Why does he feel lonely when he is surrounded by his friends and right exactly where he belongs? And why would a frog need to fly anyway?

Now, the frog feels lonelier on the ground than he did in the sky. And he spends the rest of his days waiting to be swept back up into the clouds by an unseen pair of wings. He's no longer content being a frog. Only that's what he is. He's a frog, whether he likes it or not. And that heron may or may not ever return to lift him back up.

When I think about it now, I realize it's kind of a disturb-ing fairy tale to be telling a child. I mean, what the hell? Those fishermen have a dark sensibility when you get right down to it. They get salty and a little grim out on that water, pounding Red Stripes all day long waiting for something to nibble and staring at the effortless herons who are much better fishermen than they will ever be.

My mom, probably sensing it was a pretty inappropriate story for a kid but wanting to be polite to the fishermen, would explain to me that the story was about how I should be sweet like the heron, picking up frogs, and giving them a chance to see a bigger world. She said it was the Christian thing to do, to offer your wings to those less fortunate and more landlocked than yourself. I was skeptical. I didn't think that was what the story was about at all. Mostly because I was already a frog that was dreaming of flight.

I thought a lot about that frog after my dad died. Something had happened to me, too, something that I didn't ask for, understand, or expect. And now, I could never be the same again. I would never be able to hop around the marsh grass with my friends, full of the joy of the morning, without a care in the world. And I'll always be a little in love with death.

This is the trouble with black swans. They change things forever, for no good reason, and there's not a damn thing you can do about it. You have to live the rest of your life knowing something most other people don't. It makes it hard to be close to people, which is why I had to break up with Pete. Back then, I thought it was because I shouldn't settle for the first guy I ever dated. I thought I should spread my wings a little. I thought it was his fault because he was locked up emotionally when I was going through so much. But it was all my fault. Pete was a great boyfriend. After what happened to my dad, I became stubbornly independent and singular. I think this was the ghost of my parents falling out from under me.

I was still desperately seeking a new apartment. I had to get out of my place because my feral roommates were trying to kill me. One morning, I came home from a weekend at Bev and Ben's and found that somebody had moved a beer pong table into my room. And my dad's Glock was hidden in my closet, so anybody could have taken it out to play with it. Benefield Cider House Rules: A) Guns are not toys. B) My room was strictly off-limits.

I called one of them, I can't remember which, and started

interrogating her the second she picked up. I didn't even say hello. "Listen, Cheryl or Carol or Diane, I've never said this to you, because I didn't think I needed to say something like this. I thought that this was just something people who were raised right knew without having to be told. Guess that's not you, so I'm telling you now: I don't want people in my room when I'm not home, and I definitely don't want people partying in our place right now. My dad was shot and killed, I'm grieving, and my dad's gun is in my closet, loaded. So take the party somewhere else, and stay the fuck out my stuff." Cheryl or Carol started crying and said she was sorry. I slammed down the phone mid-sob. Neither one of them came home that night, or the next, and by the third day, I'd moved out. I did not leave a note. Or the next month's rent.

After that, I moved into a frog in Mount Pleasant that belonged to a lady who had been a friend of my dad's. A *frog* is what we call an apartment down here that's built over a garage. It was bare-bones, and that's being generous. Alison, the landlady, said she wanted to do me a favor, but once I saw the place, I wasn't too sure. She only charged me four hundred a month, though, so I could live there by myself, and she let me have Sully. But it turned out to be a real hellhole. I left after only a couple of months, and my dad's concerned friend charged me two grand to repaint the joint, which I felt was a little shady. Regardless, there went the last of my savings.

After I left the frog, I moved into a studio in a complex that didn't allow dogs, on the only crappy block in all of Mount

Pleasant. You have to look pretty hard to find a low-rent district around here, but leave it to me. A couple of times, I had to step over crack vials to get to my front door. Sully went to live with Ben's dad, which broke my heart. I knew he'd be happy with Marty, though. There was a big backyard for him to run around in and other dogs for him to play with. Plus, Marty loved him like he was his own. But I missed Sully so much it hurt.

After that, I drifted, the way you do when you're sealed up in a brine pool at the bottom of the sea. I held my breath, and I waited down there, rocking back and forth in the dim tide. I didn't feel anything. The sounds of the surface world drowned in the roar of the ocean. I gave exactly zero fucks about anything. I went out drinking with my friends, moved about five more times, got through my shifts in the coffee shop every day, ate occasionally, and mostly, I slept and tried not to dream.

There was a stretch of time when I was like, *Fuck, I'm not gonna be able to do this. This fucking sucks. This is so unfair. All my friends are living their lives in college, going out partying, and blowing their money on stupid shit, and I'm sitting here, not in college, and working as a barista just barely getting by.* But every time things got really unbearable, my parents' spirits, or the universe, or God, or whoever would remind me that it was going to be okay, that everything would work out for the best, that I had to just trust the process.

One day, I stopped at a gas station. I was driving my dad's truck because I felt closer to him in it, but it cost a fortune to fill that heifer up, and it ate up gas like nobody's business. I re-alized I could only put four bucks' worth into the tank because I had exactly five bucks in my bank account, and I just broke down all of a sudden. I called my boss, Biz, sobbing.

After I had calmed down, she said, "Eva, there's a check here you never picked up. It's for like a hundred bucks." I almost fainted with relief. It's the little things like this that get you through. A kind word at just the right moment. An extra hundred bucks you didn't know you had. After she said that, I was like, *Okay, I'm going to get through this. I'm gonna make it.*

Some days, though, I have to admit, stuff gets to me no matter how hard I try to avoid it. Back then, I just couldn't climb out of the fog. I felt numb. I'd do self-destructive things to make sure I could still feel something. I was going out drink-ing way too often with my friends because at least I knew my hangovers were legit. I figured out that the haze of pain was something I could count on. One night, I cut my arm with a tomato knife. I was slicing the tomato, and then for no reason, without thinking about it really, I ran the serrated blade up my forearm from my wrist almost to the crook of my elbow. Nothing happened.

I was like, *Oh my God, I'm not even bleeding. Have I turned into a vampire?* I looked at myself in the glass on my phone to make sure I still had a reflection. Then, a few seconds later, I did start to bleed, in rivulets and estuaries waterfalling down my wrist and onto the countertop. When it started dripping onto the floor, I felt some initial relief that I was still human, and then I panicked. I ran downstairs and banged on the neighbor's door and asked her to please help me. Thank God she was home and bandaged my arm, and then Miles came over and drove me to the hospital.

Obviously, I lived.

CHAPTER 23

WHEN I GROW UP, I WANT TO BE A GHOST COWBOY

There was a lot happening that first year after my dad was killed. Once *Vanity Fair* published its article about the phony ballet and how the whole thing ended, it felt like every rag on the planet started calling, which was kind of thrilling but awful at the same time. For one thing, I didn't love the *Vanity Fair* piece. I mean, I love *Vanity Fair*, but I felt like it made my dad seem like some gun-crazy Trumper, and like Ashley had been telling the truth when I knew that all Ashley did was lie her stupid face off. They weren't even good lies. I couldn't understand why everyone didn't see right through her.

It's really a strange experience to go from being just another kid growing up in a sleepy suburban womb with an ocean view to somebody who's being interviewed by CBS and *Vanity Fair*. Reporters were calling me, asking me all kinds of really personal questions, and I tried to answer them as honestly as I could, but it was tough to know the right thing to say sometimes. And you never know what people are going to take away from it. I wanted to represent my father as he was, talk about what a good man he was, but I don't think that was the story most reporters wanted to tell.

And so, life went on. Fortunately, I really love my job at the Brown Fox, but I wasn't making enough money to pay actual real-life adult bills. I needed a real job for that. I started looking around, trying to figure out my next move, but mostly just putting one foot in front of the other. I was learning that I liked being on my own. I started thinking, like a lot of creators do, about how I could make money doing what I really loved to do.

What I really love to do is draw and paint, and I love fashion. It's hard to figure out how to make money doing art or fashion. I didn't really know where I was headed, but I just kept moving in the direction of where I thought I wanted to be. Heaven to me was to live in some old-timey shack in the Low Country, close to the fall line, where I could get up every morning and spend my day painting and surfing and playing with Sully.

It had been just over a year since my dad died. It was the second Christmas he had missed, but I don't even remember what I did for Christmas right after he passed. Christmas just didn't happen that year. So it was really the first Christmas for me without him, and my Uncle Dave didn't want me to be alone. So I went to Denton, Texas, where my dad grew up, to spend Christmas with my cousins. It was a kind of weird trip but cool, too. It was cool-weird.

One of the things you don't think about when you lose your parents when you're young is that your mom and dad are gone before you're old enough to get to know them as people. When you're a kid, they are just these authority figures telling you do your homework, and quit biting your nails, and don't smoke weed, and don't hang out with boys in tractor sheds after dark. You don't see your parents as humans until you're an adult yourself.

On that trip to Denton, I caught my first glimpse of who my dad was when he was a kid. My dad didn't talk much about his past, so I didn't know a lot about what his life was like growing up. I learned that he was popular in school—not a surprise—and that he was the guy who took charge and organized all the social events for his class. Also not a surprise. I learned that he was creative, like I am. They're big on murals down in Denton, and my cousins showed me a mural my dad painted on the side of the field house, with the sun rising up over the prairie and a lonesome cowboy riding the range. It looked like something I might have painted. That part did take me by surprise.

This made me sad about losing my dad on a whole new level. I felt a little cheated out of getting to know this guy, the young man who wanted to be an artist and who would probably have come forward and expressed himself once he didn't have so much responsibility on his shoulders. I understood now why he was such a dreamer. It made me sad, but it also made me happy to know that we were more alike than I had realized. It answered some questions, too, like why he had taught me to draw and paint, why I was allowed to buy anything I wanted to in the arts and crafts aisle at Home Depot, why he was so diligent about reminding me to always think creatively and to find my own voice.

Once I got home, I was thinking about how I really wanted to be a professional artist and how I wanted desperately to spend more time with that part of myself. And maybe people would like my work. Maybe I had some of my dad's talent. Besides, I was broke. Passionate and purposeful barista though I was, slinging coffee wasn't paying the bills, and I was over counting pennies for everything I did. I was sick of my tiny studio in an apartment complex in the only crappy neighborhood in Mount Pleasant. I was sick of having to get in my truck and drive miles to the ocean, and I was sick of life without Sully. I was ready to want things for myself again.

I wanted to live on the ocean. I wanted to wake up every morning at sunrise and watch the sunset every night over the water. I wanted to walk my dog on the beach. And all of that meant just one thing—I needed a real job. I had heard through the grapevine that a monogram company downtown was looking for a director of sales. I thought, *Hmm, sales, that's what my dad did. I bet I would be good at that, and marketing is kind of creative.* I mean, right? I figured what the hell. I had nothing to lose except a lifelong career as a barista. Here's one good thing about having the worst happen to you, twice: Sure, you're hypervigilant all the time, prone to panic and super hard on yourself, but you're also fearless, creative, and up for anything.

I knew that I really didn't have the credentials to be a director of sales. But I did have a fairly decent social media following that I'd been building since high school. That was sort of like marketing, right? Also, I knew how to be friendly and charming from working at the Brown Fox. Plus, I am Charleston born and bred, after all, and if there's one thing we know how to do down here, it's talk people into buying stuff they didn't even know they wanted.

When I got to the interview, I walked into this warehouse-looking place, with machines whirring and humming and clicking and hissing, and all turning out personalized swag. I don't know why, but I felt immediately comfortable the second I walked through the door. It was like the arts and crafts aisle on steroids. I was in the place where art gets made. It felt like home. I sat down with Greg, the guy who owned the place, and told him a little bit about my story. He told me he lost his dad young, too. It's weird how many people you meet whose parents are dead once yours are, too. It felt like a good fit to me, so I gave that job interview my best shot, and then I paced back and forth in my apartment for three days, freaking out by the phone until Greg called and offered me a job.

When he finally called, I took the offer on the spot. I did not negotiate. I did not hold out for more money or better terms. I had no leverage. It's very hard to negotiate when you've never had a real job before, only one semester of college, and your back is against the wall. I didn't get the sales director job; I was totally unqualified for that position. I knew it, and

Greg knew it. But I did come on board as the director of social media, which sounded pretty sweet to me. And the money was way better than at Brown Fox, although Biz still let me pick up shifts here and there when I needed the extra coin. Which was often.

I was quite surprised to discover that I actually liked my new job. I started to instinctively understand the way TikTok worked and began building a following there, and I was creating content for Greg's company that was sorta semi-viral. I loved thinking about what I would create that day and then just sitting down and having the tools to make it happen. One day, I stopped and noticed that for the first time in a year and a half, I hadn't even once thought about my dad dying. This was a major milestone.

TikTok was a super creative outlet for me. I started telling my story, bit by bit, only with positivity and even a little humor now and then. Yes, I cracked a few jokes about my dad getting shot, because honestly, the way stuff went down so crazy and all, some of it was so absurd, in retrospect. Some people thought I was nuts or disturbing. But others—more people, actually— got me. My dad dying isn't comedy. Obviously, I know that. But I wanted folks to know that nothing is so terrible that you can't find a way to laugh at yourself and at this crazy, fucked-up life. I mean, otherwise, what's the point?

I think that's one of the good things about social media that people don't talk about because they're so busy talking about how it destroys the self-image of teenage girls. Which of course it can and does all the time. Mine included. But social media also built me back up. It was a safe space where I felt heard and seen and even understood. People I didn't even know were rooting for me, and praying for me, and wanting me to survive. I didn't feel so much like such a freaky frog anymore. I found a pond full of frogs trying to grow wings.

The love and support that flowed to me through that portal, the stories from girls who had been through even worse stuff than I had and yet were still riding the range and stomping the fall line, happy and strong, gave me hope. Their stories encouraged me to be strong like they were and reminded me that I wasn't alone. I knew there were people out there who understood, who knew how I felt, who wanted me to move forward, to be happy again. They didn't expect me to be a mess, and they weren't put off by my resilience or my dark humor. This was really the beginning of how I started to gain the confidence I needed to think about creating my own line of wearable art. The seeds were there in the connections and community I was making on social media.

One day, I was just sitting there in my "office" with nothing to do, trying to look busy, when I thought, *Hey, Eva, here you are surrounded by T-shirt blanks and silk screens and printers and pressers and irons and embossers. What if you, who wants to be a creator, put out your own T-shirts with your art on them? What would you put on a shirt? And what kind of a shirt would sell?* I talked to Greg about it, and he was like, "Sure, make a shirt, put it on the website, and see what happens." But I just kept turning things over in my mind and doing everything but actually sitting down and making a shirt.

Finally, Greg was like, "Hey, Eva, just put out a damn shirt already. You can't sell something that exists only in your imagination." That turned out to be the most important business lesson ever. I tell everybody this who wants to start their own thing. Just put something out there and see what happens. It's not that hard. Just close your eyes, plug your nose, and dive into the water. You can't learn to swim standing on the side of the pool.

I had a pretty decent following thanks to being known as "Black Swan Murder girl," but what did I want to say now that I had the chance? I mean, besides the obvious. What mattered to me enough to put it on a shirt that other people would wear? And that's when Kanye popped into mind. I loved Kanye back then—like, so much, before he said all that stupid shit and became a crazy asshole. I loved that he was a musical genius and a fashion force. I loved that he'd made his music translate into fashion and lifestyle.

I found a picture of Kanye, one that was full-on Ye before the fall, and I drew a cute little red cowboy hat on him with gold trim. I looked at the image and thought, *You have Ye'd your last Haw. That's pretty good.* So, I put that on a shirt, using this old-timey-looking press in our shop. That machine and I have a love-hate relationship. I think it's part of what makes the shirts so interesting.

I figured I'd sell a few shirts—test out my idea, and if it worked, maybe Greg would let me do a second shirt. Honestly, I'm not that strategic. I move on impulse, and this was just a spur-of-the-moment, crazy, creative experiment kind of a thing. But inside of two hours, I swear to God, the shirt went viral. To this day, I have no idea how it happened. It was, like so many things in my life, a complete and inexplicable surprise.

I was like, *OMFG, jackpot!* For a second, I was floating on a beautiful cloud of billowy Benjamins. The next second, I was like, *Oh my God, how am I going to fulfill all these orders?* I was about to get my first lesson in how to hit the ground running and scale on the fly.

I sat down with Greg, because I knew this was now bigger than I was, and when that happens, I know enough to ask for help from people who know more than I do about handling big stuff. Second-most important lesson about starting your own brand: When you need help, ask for it, and then listen to what people who know more than you have to say about your situation. And then follow their instructions to the letter, until you know more than they do. Then it's time to move on.

Greg had been a little down in the dumps around that time. I knew that the monogram company was going through some tough times since the pandemic. It had been a couple of years by then, but COVID had permanently changed the way people hung out down here. They weren't getting together in large-enough groups to want to monogram a bunch of jackets and hats to memorialize the occasion. There were still bachelorette parties roaming through the streets in matching shirts, but they could get that stuff cheaper on Amazon. But you couldn't get my art on Amazon, and my sales had just gone through the roof.

Greg pulled out a chair and just sort of collapsed in front of me at the folding table we called my desk. "What d'ya got?"

he asked, politely uninterested. I told him what had happened with the Kanye shirt. He didn't really pay much attention. I was always going on at him about something he thought was kind of dumb, but then I showed him my numbers, and his eyes lit up. He sat up in his chair, looking over my order sheet, and I watched him un-slump before my very eyes. Then he sprang into action with the kind of upward oscillating energy I hadn't seen from him like maybe ever. It's true what they say. A rising tide really does raise all boats.

Within a couple of weeks, we'd fulfilled all those first orders, and more orders just kept flooding in. Greg looked at me and smiled. "So," he said with a goofy grin, "what's your next shirt gonna be, Picasso?" And just like that, I was on my way. I didn't know quite where I was going yet, but I didn't much care so long as I figured out how to keep going viral and making all those beautiful Benjamins appear out of the clear blue sky.

I followed up the debut Kanye design with a shirt that stayed true to my Kanye roots, but introduced a new element, based on my not-so-secret celebrity crush on Pete Davidson. I swear half the reason I dated my boyfriend Pete in the first place was because his name was Pete. That is so embarrassing to admit.

Skete was supposedly dating Kim Kardashian at the time, but I never bought into that hype. I knew that was all for publicity. My friend who knew someone who knew Pete Davidson told me not to worry. Even when I saw Pete Davidson's dogs in Kim Kardashian's yard, I wasn't fooled. I was sure that Skete was saving himself for that magical day when our eyes would meet, and he'd know, just like I always had, that we were soul-mates, destined to spend eternity together. Okay, I didn't really think that. I'm not delusional or some stalker. But I did come up with a picture of Kanye holding up those creepy stick figures he drew with Skete crossed out. And believe it or not, my second shirt ALSO WENT VIRAL.

They say that there's no time like the first time, but I'm here to tell you, the second times are even better. First times are amazing and wonderful and memorable. But doing something a second time means that first time wasn't an accident. It means you know what the hell you're doing and can do it again. That's a very good thing to know about yourself. To know that you can iterate.

"So what are you going to call your brand?" Greg asked me when the orders on the second shirt came in. "You can't be a brand unless you have a name, Eva." I started to think about that. What did I want my brand to be called? What story did I want to tell? And that's when I started thinking about my dad and that drawing he did in Denton of that old-timey cowboy riding the range in the sunset.

Ever since I was a little kid, I'd loved cowboys. I used to be a cowboy every Halloween. "Eva, don't you want to be a princess this year?" my mom would ask me hopefully.

"Nope. Cowboy," I'd say, and she'd sigh and put the tiara away for the following year. I had the whole outfit, and I'd wear it around the house even when it wasn't Halloween. I had little white cowboy boots, a western shirt, and a cute little skirt with faux-leather fringe. A red cowboy hat with gold trim, obviously.

My mom would never let me buy the toy six-shooter, though. She didn't believe in merch that made violence seem like a game. Then when I was about eight, my dad taught me to draw a ghost, and after that, all I ever wanted to draw was ghosts, only my ghosts were always cowboys. So that's what I decided to call my brand: *Ghost Cowboy*. And then I drew a logo that looked like this:

Ghost Cowboy

So now I had a name, and a logo, and the rest is Ghost Cowboy history. What? The skull part freaks you out? Well, what did you expect? A seagull and a sunrise? A single pink rose? I don't think so. That's not how I roll. After about six months of brisk Ghost Cowboy sales and less brisk sales in the monogram company, in the winter of 2022, Greg told me he wanted to talk to me and motioned for me to come into his office.

Now, I am a person who is pretty used to hearing bad news, so I know what an unpleasant surprise looks like when it calls me into the back office. I am also pretty good by now at figuring out what the bad news is, before anyone even has a chance to pronounce the words. Like in this case, I just knew that Greg was going to lay me off because the main business was down. I could practically hear how the conversation was going to go down. So I cut the bad news off at the pass.

"I have been thinking about it, and I have a proposition for you, my dude," I said.

"Okay, I'm listening," Greg said, although he clearly was not listening but instead was dreading laying me off and crunching the crumbs from an almost empty bag of Funyuns. I had been watching him stress-eat shit for a week. And lately, he always looked hungover.

"How's about I work for you for free?" I said extremely cheerfully, like my dad used to do when he was hard-selling a dicey idea. "How about I come to work for you for nothing? As in, you don't have to pay me."

At this point, he looked up, put down the Funyuns, and started to pay attention. "What's the catch?" he asked, suspicious of my inexplicable and irrational generosity.

"No catch," I said. "I'll come in and work every day just like always. You don't pay me. I'm a separate company. But in exchange for me working for you for free, you let me build my brand using your equipment. What do you say? Do we have a deal?"

"Deal," Greg said, and we shook hands.

"So now what did you want to talk to me about?"

"Oh, nothing. It's not important now," Greg said. "Numbers are a little down, but we'll pick back up. We'll turn things around with a little help from Ghost Cowboy." He put his arm around me awkwardly, leaving Funyun crumbs on my sleeve. Months later, he would threaten to sue me and try to take my brand. But I stopped him cold with a little help from a new business manager and a very expensive legal team. So don't let the cute crumbs fool you. Greg was a shark in a Funyun wrapper.

CHAPTER 24

SLOW DANCING
IN THE COURTHOUSE

It took four long years to bring Ashley to trial. And there were so many interminable delays and legal traffic jams along the way. It was excruciating, because on a certain level, until that trial happened, I couldn't move on. The story was still ongoing, and I was so ready for a new chapter. Finally, in the summer of 2023, three years after my dad was killed, Suzanne, the assistant district attorney, called to tell me that Ashley had filed for stand-your-ground immunity and was trying to have her murder 2 charges thrown out because she was acting in self-defense and something something castle law.

Suzanne told me there was a hearing scheduled in just a few weeks, and if Ashley won, she'd be off the hook completely. I couldn't even wrap my head around that. How could she get off scot-free when my dad was dead? If she won, the case would never go to trial, and she would never be held accountable. And where would that leave me, exactly?

"Wait." It was sinking in what she was saying to me. "You mean she could get off completely? How could that happen? I mean, she shot my unarmed dad when he was trying to get away from her. I thought this was an open-and-shut case."

"Well, in the state of Florida, you're allowed to shoot an intruder in your home, if you're in reasonable fear for your life."

I couldn't quite understand how my dad could be an intruder. He was packing the house for them because they were all moving to Maryland. The house was totally empty, except for Ashley's three loaded guns that were stashed around the house, not including the one she used to shoot my dad. And I'm pretty sure my dad paid their rent, so NOT an intruder.

"I wouldn't worry too much about this, Eva," Suzanne said, like she'd seen all this before a thousand times and probably would see a thousand more. "This is just another bend in the road. She's not going to win. Judge Whyte is very thorough and very reasonable. He'll get to the truth. No need to worry about this. I'm not."

I spent the next month mentally preparing myself to attend the hearing and getting ready to see Ashley for the first time since that terrible Christmas when she told me my dad had murdered my mother. Suzanne had said I didn't have to be there, but there was no way I was missing my first chance to look Ashley in her face. For over three years, I had been waiting to ask her, *My God, Ashley, how could you do this to me?*

For three years, the question had preoccupied me. How could she have done this when she knew my mom was dead?

Why would she kill my father and leave me with no parents? She lost her own father when she was fifteen, so she knew what it was like to grow up without a father. And now she had done the same thing to Emerson and me. Even after everything I came to understand about the situation between Ashley and my dad, I just did not get it. I still don't.

Once I knew the hearing was approaching, I became completely preoccupied imagining what it would be like to see Ashley again. I wanted to see her see me. I wanted to look in her face and show her, *Yes, I'm a real human being, and you, you did this terrible thing to me.* I think I wanted to know that she felt some remorse for taking away the one person I loved most in the world. I wanted to see that she saw my pain, that she was sorry.

After my dad was killed, and then Ashley was arrested, everybody, including Suzanne, had told me I could not reach out to her, even though I wanted to so badly. It was a mutual no-contact order. If Ashley talked to me, or even messaged me over social media, she would violate her surety bond, and they'd send her back to jail. Suzanne told me if I reached out, I could jeopardize the case, so I resisted. For all that time, I stayed quiet. I waited patiently, like a heron, for justice to arrive. And when it finally did, it came in a rush.

When I was a kid, my dad took me to Washington, DC, with him on a business trip once, and we took a tour of the Supreme Court. What an echoey, timeless, ponderous, snack stand–less place that was. My dad pointed out all the lion heads in the architecture. He told me that lions were a symbol of justice, fierce and royal and swift—the king of beasts. But at the base of the pillars were tortoises, one of the slowest and most deliberate creatures in the marsh. It's a contradiction that you only understand once you've been through the judicial system.

How would I feel when I saw her? What would she look like now? What outfit should I wear? I was still a kid the last time she saw me. I wanted her to see me now that I had grown up despite her. I wanted her to realize that I had won because I survived. I was still here to tell the truth.

The hearing was at the end of July 2023 on a Monday. I drove down with my bestie, Taylor, and Mame, my yoga teacher, who were both so generous to come with me, because I really needed their support. My Cousin Tommie and my Uncle Dave and my cousins were going to be there, too, and, of course, Stephanie, my dad's lawyer from Florida who was going to testify about the custody case and all the crazy stuff Ashley had done to my dad through the family courts. Mame and Taylor and I got our own Airbnb because I thought I should carve out a safe space for myself. I didn't know what to expect from the hearing or from myself. I wanted just my close circle of trust around me.

When I walked into the courtroom, Ashley was already seated up front at the defense table with her lawyer. I could see when her shoulders went up to her ears that she could sense my presence, but she never turned around to look at me. It would have been hard for anybody with even a trace of survival in-stinct not to feel me. I was staring holes in the back of her head with the white-hot intensity of a thousand suns.

ADA Suzanne, perhaps fearing I would burst into flames at any moment, walked up from the prosecutor's table and put her hand on my shoulder. "Are you okay, Eva?" she asked, and I nodded, even though I didn't really know how I felt. "Now remember, sweetie," she said, "there's going to be some autopsy pictures of your dad I'm going to show in my argument, and they will be upsetting. I don't have to put them up on the overhead if you don't want me to. I can just hand them to the judge, and you won't have to see them. The only trouble with that is, the media won't see them either if I do that."

"Put them up on the screen. I want everyone to see," I said, with a little bit more confidence than I probably should have felt, given what happened later. Suzanne patted me on the back then and smiled, but looked skeptical. She knew what was coming, and I did not.

"You can always leave the courtroom if it's too upsetting. Just get up and walk on out into the hall. Go grab yourself a coffee or something; there's a real good coffee place right next door."

Hmm. She had prescribed coffee. In advance. Maybe this was a bigger deal than I thought. Maybe I should have told her not to show those pictures. Maybe they were really epically and historically gruesome. "Just be sure to warn me before, okay?" I asked.

"Sure thing," Suzanne said, and rushed back on her power pumps to the prosecutors' table and began conferring with her colleague. Then the judge, who seemed calm and fair and reasonable and even a little pastoral like my Uncle Dave, read the complaint.

Ashley's lawyer got up to give her side of the argument, and the minute he called my dad an abuser in open court, I felt myself leaving my body. Fortunately or unfortunately, he droned on so long, the boredom reestablished a weird kind of normalcy, and I reintegrated. Then finally, Suzanne got up and spoke for my dad and began to call witnesses. I braced for impact on landing.

The courtroom wasn't very fancy. Just a lot of faux wood paneling and a judge's bench and the seal of the great state of Florida. Cousin Tommie took the stand first and looked a little nervous, but he did a great job. He painted a picture of my dad as a navy pilot and a dedicated officer, a.k.a. not a wife-beating, child-molesting, gun-toting Trumper. Then Stephanie was called to the stand, and through her testimony, laid out the timeline of the custody proceedings. All the puzzle pieces I'd only seen in bits and pieces came together into a picture of what sounded like a surprisingly sophisticated plot to get rid of my dad. And Ashley had succeeded, while the whole time, my dad had just kept telling us all that everything was fine.

Next, CSI got up and talked about the trajectory of the bullets, which got very technical and boring. That's how trials are a little like life. They are moments of pure terror or exhilaration mixed with complete and utter boredom. Terror meets torpor. There were diagrams showing where Ashley and my dad would have been standing when she pulled the trigger. Then without warning me, Suzanne flashed up those crime scene and autopsy pictures—larger-than-life snaps of my dad bleeding all over Ashley's bedroom floor and then a snap of my dad lying naked on a cooling table in the morgue, with a toe tag on his foot.

These images exploded onto the screen and burned them-selves into my brain forever. The last one I saw was my dad with a hole in his chest and blood all over his face, dead as a doornail. That's when I had had enough. I got up and left the courtroom, heading for the coffee shop next door. I'm still not sure why, but after three years of being numb about pretty much everything, those pictures unleashed a flood of feels. The levee inside me broke, and the water rushed in. I realized in a way that I hadn't before that both my parents were 150 percent dead and gone. I wouldn't be seeing them anymore. Then I ugly cried into my cold brew for a few minutes and shot a reel of my uneaten salad. Then I posted it, because that's what you do when you're the CEO of OrphanTok. I got over a million views in about half an hour. So weird.

When the court recessed for lunch, I was determined to get Ashley to look me in the eye, and I knew this was my last chance. I waited by the exit and watched her as she made her way slowly up the aisle, like if she walked slowly enough, I'd give up and leave before she got there. I was determined. She wasn't going to avoid me. I was right in the middle of the only exit. I stood there, and I waited, staring holes in her head. Fi-nally, she looked at me briefly before brushing right past me. Her face was expressionless. If anything, she looked vaguely an-noyed with me. Like it was all my fault, just like always. Yeah, that bitch hated me from the jump.

Our side took up the rest of the day, and it was a long dirge with very little comic relief. You know you're in trouble when the medical examiner is the funniest act of the day. That first day exhausted me, and so as I made my way to the courtroom the next day, in an oversized black jumper, I was feeling pretty sick to my stomach. I knew I would be sitting through eight hours of hate speech about my dad that day and would have to sit there quietly and just take in all the lying about my dad and me, even about my mom. I was like, *Girl, keep my mom's name out of your mouth.*

And then, without Ashley ever saying anything at all, or calling any witnesses, the defense abruptly rested. I could hardly believe it. Ashley did not testify, although she was claiming self-defense. She thought she could get immunity without ever telling anybody her version of the story. Only her lawyer presented an argument, and everybody knows that's not evidence. Her lawyer rattled on about case law and statutes and a whole bunch of stuff I didn't understand for what seemed like hours. The prosecutor and the judge also looked confused by the meandering argument, and I took that as a good sign. Then Suzanne got up for final summation, and the judge adjourned without making a ruling. More waiting and holding my breath. Great!

Three months later, Ashley's motion for immunity was denied because she didn't testify, which meant she failed to present any real evidence. A trial date was set for the following summer. Another whole year of life to live while I waited for justice to crawl toward me on the back of a turtle.

CHAPTER 25

I WANT TO MARRY
A LIGHTHOUSE KEEPER

No offense whatsoever to Skete or my latest obsession, the transcendent and in my view criminally under-rated Dominic Fike, but I always thought it would be awesome to marry a lighthouse keeper. We would live by the side of the sea in one of those tall towers with the spiral staircases that spin all the way up to the top, where you can step outside and take in the whole breadth and sweep of Charleston Bay.

Chucktown was the first commercial port in the whole country, so the lighthouses around here have some serious wattage. It's like tradition or something. The old lighthouse on Sullivan's Island was as bright as twenty-eight million candles, and the light stretched a full twenty-six miles out to sea. That's a pretty amazing innovation considering the first lighthouse around here was a burning barrel on the beach at Morris Island.

Of course, lighthouse keepers are hard to find these days, as most lighthouses are fully automatic, which I think is kind of tragic. Automatic lighthouses are not poetic, lyrical, or even haunted, which is an embarrassment around here. No resident ghost. There used to be a lighthouse keeper on Morris Island. Originally, that lighthouse had its own microcommunity, with three houses—a big three-story mansion for the keeper and his family and two smaller places for his assistants. There were a couple of barns for the animals, a vegetable garden, chicken coops, even a one-room schoolhouse for the kids. My dude was all set up out there.

I could have married that lighthouse keeper and lived the rest of my life out there in the middle of the bay, right on the fringed hem of the continent, cut off but completely self-sufficient. Unfortunately, the Morris Island lighthouse got wiped out in an earthquake. Then after Hugo, all that was left was the dock, and then Irma came and took care of even that. Eventually, the state bought the place for a dollar, and now it's gone dark. When I marry Dominic Fike, we're gonna buy the place back and restore it and install an old-timey Fresnel that will shine way farther and brighter than any of the modern, automatic lighthouses. And then we'll just live there and have a family, and I'll paint all day long until it's time to make supper and put the kids to bed.

People have been trying to find their way around Charleston in the dark for centuries. They paint church steeples around here white so people can navigate to their home port drunk after nightfall. I'm not even kidding. It's a city of light and darkness and bourbon, all running right into one another on every street corner. My friend Miles works on a tugboat. He works two weeks a month and gets paid for the whole month. That part is hard to beat. Half the month, he's out on the water working, and then for two weeks, he's home doing nothing at all and getting paid for it. The money is pretty good, but the work is really hard. Plus, you have to be on a small boat with a bunch of big idiots, and you get drug tested all the time. This would rule me out. I get PTSD whenever I have to pee in a cup.

About a month after the immunity hearing, Miles called me during his week onshore and told me he had found a cute two-bedroom house by the beach on Isle of Palms, and did I want to come and take a look? Miles was still living with his folks, and it was definitely time for him to bust a move. Once you start hitting twenty-two, twenty-three, he told me, you've got to fly the nest. I wouldn't know about leaving the nest. My nest left me.

I told Miles I'd go look at the house with him. I figured if it worked out, I'd have a roommate that would be gone half the time, and I could have the house to myself for those weeks. Sounded like a sweet setup. I could be a lone wolf, and then by the time I got lonely banging around the house by myself, Miles would be home. Plus, maybe Sully could live with me again. So why not at least go and look at it. It was on the beach, so I couldn't say no, right?

Of course, the place was adorable, and I fell in love with it instantly. It's damn near impossible to find an affordable cottage by the beach. It felt like it was a gift from my parents, who knew how I felt about the ocean, and when that kind of miracle crosses your threshold, it would be very impolite not to let it in and offer it a glass of sweet tea. I fell in absolute love with the place. We applied on the spot. And so for days after, I paced the room and tried to regulate my breathing until we got approved.

In the interim, I called my Uncle Dave and asked him what he thought about the idea. "I'd have to break my lease at the complex, which would mean paying double rent for a few months," I told him and then waited to hear what he had to say, although I had a pretty good idea of how he was going to feel about this plan.

"That doesn't sound like the most sensible idea to me, Eva," he said predictably. "Aren't you having a tough time paying one rent, and now you want to pay two?" He was right, of course, and he wasn't. I explained my reasoning and showed him I'd done the math, and then he told me I should go into sales, because I had almost convinced him that my dumb idea was the smart move. And that's how I wound up in the beach cottage of my dreams on Isle of Palms. The next day, I broke my lease. It wasn't even really a question. I know what I want when I see it. And if my parents' deaths taught me anything, it's what are you waiting for, fool? If you know what you want, go get it, because if you wait, it might be too late.

The day we moved in, we got all the big stuff hauled inside, and then I went to pick up Sully. He was so excited to see me, he almost knocked me right off my feet. Then he jumped up next to me in the whip, just like always, and he basically didn't leave my side for like, well, he hasn't left it yet. I love him so much. We said goodbye to Marty, and I thanked him for taking such good care of my buddy, and he told me he was glad to have Sully around. Marty looked sad to see us both go. Well, Sully had been with him for almost a year while I found my feet, but he told me he was happy to know that Sully and I were going to be together again, that Sully and I were going to be right where we belonged.

And then Sully and I moved into our little bungalow by the sea. We both love the beach, which is a good thing, because outside of work and yoga, and the occasional stomp around town with friends, that's where you'll find us. Once I moved onto Isle of Palms, I was never very far from the sea. I had bubbled and rushed my way back to my source. And like centuries of old-timey girlies before me, I would sit on that shoreline by the lighthouse, looking out to sea, waiting for my true love to come sailing into harbor after his latest world concert tour. Also, I surf. And stuff Jiffy bags with T-shirts. I do this a lot.

I worked hard building my Ghost Cowboy brand and speed-learning how to be an adult. I also started working on this book, which was cathartic and healing. It felt freeing and wonderful and sometimes painful to tell my story. I did this so I could be a lighthouse for other lost ships like me. Taylor came to work with me, and we got even tighter than we were already, which was hard to imagine. I don't know what I would have ever done without her friendship.

I still thought about my parents all the time. With my mom, it was the little things I would come across during my day. A daffodil, or folding a napkin like a seashell the way she taught me, or rushing around in eight directions when I can only accomplish four, or when I look in the mirror. My thoughts about my dad were different, unsettled and raw. Until Ashley was in jail, he would be a sad ghost walking.

It had taken so long for my dad to get the justice he deserved. I thought, if justice were a feeling, it would be like when you close a lid on a treasure chest and then chuck it into the ocean. You know it's there, you know it's locked up safe, but you can't get to it. Not until you venture to the bottom of the sea.

I feel like I'm always standing in between two worlds, the one before and the one after, the one that was and the one that is only just coming into view. In a way, I'm just like all the other kids around here, trying to figure myself out, having fun with my friends, starting to build a career I'm not quite clear on yet, trying to find my person and fall in love. But in another way, I'm not like anybody else I know. I don't have the same options that they do. I can't live with my parents while I figure out what I want to do with my life. I can't call my mom when I'm sick or when my heart gets broken. I can't call my dad for advice or to see if he wants to take me fishing or lend me twenty bucks when I run short. But I do have one thing still—I have the Low Country, where I can hear God speaking to me.

There are lots of *I can'ts* in my life. I can't go home for Christmas. My parents will never wish me happy birthday or watch me walk down the aisle at my wedding or hold my first child. I can't lean on them. I can't make them proud. I can't show them what a good job they did bringing me up. But both my parents would tell me to focus not on the dead things but on what's still alive. And that's what I did, and that's what I still do. I focus on the living things. Back then, I was singularly focused on my artwork, on Ghost Cowboy, on writing this book, on building my independence, on hanging on to my sense of humor, on loving the hell out of my little cottage by the beach, and on playing Frisbee in the surf with my fabulous, sloppy golden retriever who had finally come home. And that's not nothing. That's everything.

CHAPTER 26

TWO TEARS IN A BUCKET, MOTHERFUCK IT

It's weird when you've imagined something happening for such a long time and then it happens, and it turns out to be nothing at all like what you'd thought. I had been dreaming about Ashley's trial for four long years, and I thought I knew exactly how things were going to go. Yet the moment I walked into that courtroom, I knew I had been wrong about all of it. I had no idea what this experience was going to be like. I was a stranger in a strange land.

There was no stately courtroom. No big mahogany bench. No big gavel banging the world to order, no statues of fierce lions. Just a simple and not at all extraordinary courtroom, in some bog water in central Florida, where you could not find a decent chicken wing or fried oyster for two hundred miles in any direction.

In the days leading up to the trial, the poor suckers from Ashley's church were protesting out in front of the courthouse, convinced that Ashley was some kind of a battered mom who had slayed the abusive monster to protect herself and her child. They had signs shouting STAND WITH ASHLEY and SELF-DEFENSE IS NOT A CRIME, which was so much bullshit I could barf. I saw on the local news that my baby sister, Emerson, was out there, too, holding up a sign that said LET MY MOMMY BE FREE. I hope somebody has started a GoFundMe to pay for that poor kid's future therapy.

This is when I realized Ashley wasn't just a killer, she was also a super-bad mom. She had been a uniquely untalented stepmom, too. But watching her make her six-year-old daughter protest in defense of the slaying of her own dad was just beyond Freudian. I felt so bad for the little sister who might grow up hating me, without ever knowing me.

The bailiffs had cleared the front of the courthouse on the first day of trial. You can't have a jury pool passing through that kind of misguided human propaganda trooping up and down the sidewalk. I was so relieved when they finally left. Those people had been fooled, just like a lot of the people littering the shoulders on the road up Mount Ashley—my dad included. I didn't feel sorry for them. It infuriated me to watch them supporting a liar while being so righteous and certain that they were doing the Lord's work. Which they definitely were not.

That whole first day was taken up by jury selection, which was sweet because Taylor and I were free to explore downtown Bradenton, where we discovered pretty quickly it was impossible to find anything to do or see or even eat within walking distance of the courthouse. I think we wound up back in our Airbnb with a bottle of Aperol, a six-pack of Pellegrino, and a bag of chips. Suzanne called at the end of the day to tell me a jury had been selected. So the very next morning, it was go time.

The only good thing I can say about that morning was that I was more used to the proceedings this time, so it wasn't as surreal as the immunity hearing. I don't know what I was expecting specifically at trial, but whatever it was, the reality was like a cheap knockoff of the version I had been harboring in my imagination. It was slow and methodical, and so much of it seemed beside the point.

I realized that it didn't matter anymore why Ashley had killed my dad. Now, it was just about settling the bill. I had to be cool with that. I had to let all my questions go, and even the anger. Being pissed at Ashley for the rest of my life wouldn't do anybody any good, and it wouldn't bring my dad back.

Ashley was poised on the edge of her seat at the defense table, dressed up like a trad wife with a Peter Pan collar and supertight braids that were meant to distract the jury from looking into her cold, dead eyes. The braids didn't soften her. They only made her look more severe. She never once looked up at anybody. She kept her eyes cast down, like Joan of Arc. She was cheesy as fuck right to the end. She whispered demurely to her lawyer now and then, and for the rest of the time, she sat quietly, awaiting her fate with pretend grace, embracing full victimhood, which was completely on brand.

"All rise," the bailiff barked. I took a deep breath, and then the wheels of justice began to grind.

I learned that the state always starts first in a criminal trial, so Suzanne began her opening statement, firing off a breathless and relentless timeline that laid everything out in an automatic round of fact bullets that made it clear to everybody (I hoped) what Ashley had been up to all along. She wanted sole custody of Emerson and to disappear my dad. Tommie was the prosecution's first witness. I think Suzanne wanted him to lead us off because he'd done so well in the immunity hearing, but things didn't go as planned. On cross, Ashley's attorney suggested that Tommie was in love with Ashley, because in Ashley's world, I mean, who wasn't? He misquoted some of Tommie's texts to make it seem like Tommie was flirting with Ashley while my dad was still alive, which of course wasn't true, and totally didn't matter, but just the suggestion, lie that it was, made Tommie look a little sus.

The judge admonished Ashley's lawyer, but Tommie got rattled, and the power of his testimony was sort of lost in the mud. At a certain point during a trial, you realize that getting at the truth in a courtroom is like looking through a glass darkly. Facts are doled out in tiny and contested granules, like a mandala, precisely created grain by grain, and then destroyed in the first stiff updraft. You have no idea until the very end how the jury will put the pieces together, and by the time you see the full picture, it's gone. I couldn't tell what the jury was thinking. I kept trying to read their thoughts, but they were as inscrutable and unpredictable as the undertow.

I testified right after Tommie. Tough act to follow. I heard my name called, and I raised my hand, swore to tell the truth, and settled into my chair on the stand. And I have to tell you, even though I had been preparing for this moment for literally years, when I finally got up there, I got tongue-tied like I used to when I was a kid, and my dad wasn't there to coax the words. But I needn't have worried. My time up there was painfully brief. I barely got to say five words.

After all I'd been through in that house, with my face pressed against the glass looking in at my dad's toxic marriage, I only got to answer four pretty nonessential questions. The rules of evidence prevented most of my eyewitness testimony. I didn't see Ashley shoot my dad, so really, what did I know about any of it at the end of the day? What could I say except I loved my father, and he was kind and a great dad? It occurred to me that my dad really had done a pretty good job of keeping me clear of the crazy after all. He had protected me, even though it hadn't felt like it in the moment. He had done such a good job that I couldn't really testify in his defense. His final sacrifice for me.

I had so much to say, it was practically filling up my head and spilling out the top. How long had I dreamed of my moment to proclaim the truth and vanquish my enemies, and exonerate my dad in front of the whole world? How many times had I gone over and over in my head what I wanted to say? Hundreds, maybe thousands of times before falling asleep. And I got to say none of it. So much buildup and then *swoosh*. Nothing. Story of my life.

Being involved in a murder trial isn't like what I thought it would be at all. It's not like you see on TV, where a witness takes the stand and lays down the straight poop, and the courtroom is riveted as everyone's eyes are opened at last and finally the truth is revealed, the guilty are prosecuted, the innocent are exonerated, and reason is restored. There aren't any compelling arguments or stunning reveals. No gripping reversals. Just facts, fought over, whittled down and desiccated as old deer pellets on a parched prairie.

Witness after witness got up on the stand and offered their chiseled-down nugget of truth and then exited the stage. It was a lot of mounting tension with no denouement. No moral at the end of the story. Just the whirring of old wheels going down a broken and obsolete track across a barren wasteland.

On the third day of trial, as soon as I walked into the courtroom, the defense attorney, who I was now calling *Mr. Burns* in my head, was already up on his feet droning on, complaining to Judge Whyte about something. Judge Whyte was furrowing his brow and looking concerned. I got a pit in my stomach as I entered. All eyes turned to look right at me. Apparently, Mr. Burns had been complaining about me.

Next thing I knew, I was back up on the stand, getting grilled by the judge about my TikTok videos. Old man Burns was complaining that I had violated my subpoena and spoken to the press. He literally wanted to grab my phone and look at it right there in open court. When the judge wouldn't allow an invasion of my privacy, he tried to get me barred from the courtroom for the duration. He wanted me thrown out of my own dad's murder trial. The judge said no, because of Marsy's law, and let me off with an admonishment. He said I could stay, but he made me promise to steer clear of the press and stay off TikTok. I said I would, and I did. I, unlike some people, don't lie to judges.

After that, I had to peace out for the rest of the day. I needed a break or I thought I might implode from the stress. If there's one thing I've learned in my life, it's how to get when the getting is good. I was feeling pretty vulnerable after being yelled at over nothing by a judge when it shouldn't have been me who was on trial. All I missed were the crime techs testifying, and the medical examiner, who traveled with those horrific autopsy photos in his bag. That was an experience I didn't need to endure twice. I had been seeing those pics of my dad with a toe tag in my dreams ever since the immunity hearing.

On the fourth day, Ashley shocked the courtroom by taking the stand and testifying for the very first time. I was not surprised. I knew she had been building to this grand finale. She thought she could talk her way out of this. She had thought so all along. She had supposedly told no one about the facts of that night, not even her mother, which I found less than credible. When Ashley was feeling something, everybody heard about it. Repeatedly. She would stub her toe and the mailman knew about it.

I had guessed that morning that she was planning on taking the stand, because of her churchy fit. She was dressed in a

Carolina blue twin set and a bracelet that looked like Emerson had made. Her hair was swept loosely back. She looked ready to marry Christ. She got on the stand and seated herself quietly in front of the mic, eyes downward, lips quivering, eyelashes batting, breath catching, her fake boobs hidden from sight. Then she started to sob out her side of the story. I was not surprised or even that interested in what Ashley was saying. I'd heard that old song many, many times before, and the ending was always the same.

I have to give it to her. She did paint a pitiful portrait until she opened her mouth and proceeded to chew up the scenery like it was underripe cantaloupe. She shook, she grimaced, she shuddered, she fake cried non-tears. She went through mounds of Kleenex that never got wet. The lies were just so obvious, and yet I was worried. Ashley was very manipulative. She was a terrible actress, but would the jury know that? After all, my dad, who I really respected, never figured out that he had fallen in love with death.

Ashley's testimony felt like it went on for hours, days, centuries even. She never seemed to get tired of blaming my dad for everything, for the terrible results of her own disastrous choices. She took responsibility for nothing. Instead, Ashley blamed us, me, my dad, even Tommie, for her acts of violence, large and small. As I listened to her litany that day, I realized that every single one of her accusations was a confession. I had seen her in action. I knew what she did; even though I wasn't there, I knew. And she knew I knew. But what would the jury think? Would they swallow this hook? Or would they see the true face of the redfish?

Looking back, I realize these moments are so hard to describe. They're singular and rare. Vocabulary fails. When you're out on the water, and you see a wave coming toward you, it gets bigger and bigger, and every second, it gets closer and gains heft. I expected to feel numb, or faint, or at least oxygen deprived. But instead, I felt alive. The fabric of time became structural, holding shape beneath my fingers and becoming four-dimensional.

Finally, after Ashley had dramatized her way to the end of her direct testimony, Suzanne got up to cross, and by then, I was so there for it. Suzanne immediately made Ashley get down off the stand and act out the events of that final night. I could see immediately that this made Ashley incredibly uncomfortable. It threw her completely off her game. She hadn't thought to work out her blocking. She froze, her eyes saucer-like, wrapping her arms around herself, filling in the blanks with more unimaginative and redundant sobbing. It was amazing, watching the truth radiate throughout her limbs, animating the fakeness of her story. The body doesn't lie. It's one thing to lie with your words. It's much harder to get your body language to back you up.

Mr. Burns tried to clean up Ashley's bad dance, but the damage had been done, although the DV victims on YouTube were triggered and ratio'd Suzanne in the chats. All the forensics, all the investigators and medical examiners, in other words, all the facts and evidence spoke to me with one voice. Ashley shot my unarmed dad because she wanted sole custody of their daughter. I knew for a fact that my dad would not have let Emerson grow up without him. He wanted more than anything to be her dad. And he believed to his dying day that the healing power of his love could save Ashley from herself.

After the grand finale, Ashley had just a couple of witnesses to speak for her—her mom, the delulu therapist she'd moved in with after her arrest, some old guy they paid as an expert who did not sound like any kind of expert to me, and the next-door neighbor who I'm pretty sure had a serious crush on Ashley. Her case was as flimsy as her plans for building God's ballet, drawn on heart-shaped sticky notes with those fucking colored pencils.

Closing arguments went on for what seemed like a full geological epoch. I blame Mr. Burns, who definitely graduated from the more-is-more school of law back in 1893. He was a man of many, many words, repeated slowly and often three times for emphasis. Mercifully, at about 4:00 p.m. on that last afternoon of the fifth day of trial, the case went to the jury. Taylor and I hung out in the hallway outside the courtroom trying to kill time dead with our bare hands. One hour, then two, then three, four hours went by. I drank so much coffee I thought I was going to jump right out of my skin.

The suspense was literally killing me. People say that as an expression, but I legit thought I might just dissolve into a mist. Finally, a note came out from the courtroom, and I could hardly breathe as we filed back in to hear what had happened.

But there wasn't a verdict, only a note from the foreman letting us know that the jury was having trouble reaching a verdict.

My heart leaped right into my mouth. Was it going to be another four years waiting for the excruciatingly slow hand of justice to point its unmoving finger at the truth? I could not even go there. Neither could the judge. He sent them back to deliberate some more, even though it was well on to 9:00 p.m. by then, and we all resumed our positions on the cold, hard benches and settled in for another long wait.

Then only about forty-five minutes later, the jury came back again, this time with a decision. My knees were almost knocking as the bailiff called us back into the courtroom and we waited for the jury to return. I felt this profound mix of emotions I can't even describe. I was gripping Taylor's hand so hard I thought I might cut off her circulation. She pulled her hand away and shook it to get the blood flowing again, laughed, and then grabbed my hand again. Do you see why she's my bestie?

In those long, crystalline moments right before fate walks through your front door, you run through all the feels. They all registered, pure and sequential, in a syncopated song of loss. Grief for my dad. Grief for my mom. Grief for my family life. Grief for my fractured childhood. Grief for Emerson. And then, the jury spoke.

CYPRESS TREES BELIEVE IN GOD

Ashley was found guilty of manslaughter with a firearm, a lesser included offense, which was fine by me. It wasn't murder 2 like we had hoped and felt was justified, but justice can be a crapshoot. Ashley was sentenced to twenty years in prison, and ten years' probation, which felt like justice to me. Emerson will be older than I am now by the time Ashley gets out, I wish her all the best in life, and I hope that one day, I get the chance to know my sister.

On the way home from Bradenton after the trial, I drove up north toward Florence to visit my mom's grave. I hadn't been back since we buried her. At first it was too hard, and then later, so chaotic. I think I was waiting for something, and now here it was. I brought some of my dad's ashes so I could put them next to her. I also brought a big bunch of sunflowers because, I mean, why fight the inevitable? I thought about my mom down there, sleeping in the earth like a paperwhite, waiting to pop up in spring. I made a note to plant some bulbs next time I visited so they could multiply underground and come up every year.

It's a beautiful spot, now that I was able to notice. I couldn't see past the shadow of my own grief at my mom's funeral. But now I could understand why my dad chose this spot. My mom rests on the crest of a sweeping green glen, and at the bottom was a perfect stand of cypress trees, standing sentinel, right at the border of the marsh. My mom used to tell me that cypress trees believed in God. That may be true. But more importantly, I think that cypress trees trust the process. They're self-sufficient. Resourceful. Of course they are. They're literally wood made out of water.

To survive in the Low Country, we all—plants and animals, fish and crabs and bugs and birds and trees and people, too— need to learn how to adapt. Everything changes. You just can't count on anything to stay the same. From the moment my mom died, for me, everything's been in flux. But it's settled down— for now. My business is taking off, and I am my own boss and a working artist, and I finished this book. The water has receded. But this, too, will change. I know that, and I will be ready.

There are streams and ponds and rivers and lakes within oceans, way down there at the bottom of the sea, where you can't see them. You will be moved through the river of your life by unseen currents that are bigger and more powerful than you are. Sometimes you have to rest and let the water carry you. But remember, what you don't know can hurt you.

When you're living in a soggy place like the Low Country, one of the most fragile and yet durable ecosystems on earth, you have to trust the forces of nature, because they are smarter than you are. It might not always feel good. It can definitely get uncomfortable. Sometimes to live is to suffer; that's just how it is. At those times, you have to find meaning in the pain, have faith that the pain will one day become an even greater capacity to feel joy.

And whatever you do, try to hold on to your sense of humor. Laughter is the lighthouse. Water will always get into the places you don't want it to go. It will fill up every nook and cranny. It will smash through your windows and bust down your walls. You're gonna have to learn to live with that. Because you can't fight it. But if you go with it, it'll make you the strongest substance on earth. Just like the cypress trees.

Cypress trees grow up all by themselves without any help from anybody. They rise, clean and tall out of the primordial muck. They grow straight toward the sun out of that stinky black water and become green and lush and sweet-smelling and point straight toward heaven. Those are the kind of miracles that are possible in the marsh.

Cypress trees have learned to trust the water, and the water has taught the cypress trees how to rely on themselves. They plant themselves, they feed and water themselves; they even blossom and reproduce without any help. Without anybody starting a GoFundMe account for them. They are left on their own to face the elements, the droughts and the floods and the hurricanes. And yet there are cypress trees down here that are over a thousand years old.

Some people say that cypress trees were here before the

continents even divided two hundred million years ago and formed the Charleston Bay. But even cypress trees die eventually, and when they do, they don't just slouch back into the ooze. They stand, even hundreds of years later, like a ghost forest, providing a harbor for baby fish and snakes, salamanders, and dragonflies, and all the terrible and wonderful creatures in the marsh. The ghosts of the cypress groves create an underwater nursery, where God hides, waiting to surprise you with new life.

The End

ACKNOWLEDGMENTS

To my friendly ghost and collaborator, Bev West, thank you for helping me navigate some difficult memories as we worked on this book together over these many years. I feel so lucky to have found someone who not only understands and shares my sense of humor but who was also able to help me translate my thoughts into words that I hope many will relate to. One of the few silver linings of having to go through what I went through has been befriending you in the process of sharing my story with the world.

To my intrepid agent, Kirsten Neuhaus at Ultra Literary. Thank you from the bottom of my heart for your graceful and reassuring presence and keen navigational skills on this long and winding road. You were there to get me around every bump in the road, every unexpected plot twist. Here's to traveling a more normal stretch of highway together from here on out!

A very special thanks to my equally intrepid and brilliant editor, Lauren Spiegel. I'm so grateful for your thoughtful and careful stewardship and your unflagging belief in me and in this book. No first-time author could have asked for a better sherpa.

Thanks to Aimee Bell, and to Taylor Rondestvedt, for their amazing assist, stepping seamlessly into the action whenever we needed it most. Thanks also to Sarah Wright and Emily Arzeno and finally to the iconic Gray Hamner for the artful glow up.

Finally, thank you to ASA Suzanne O'Donnell and ASA Rebecca Freel for their support, and their unwavering and passionate commitment to securing a just outcome for my dad. Thanks also to His Honor Judge Matt Whyte, who gave us all a fair shake and reassured me that in the end, justice really does prevail.

To my family and friends—where would I be without you? To my uncles Dave and Wes, also Roxy, Cassie, John, and Brooke, thank you for reminding me every day that we Benefields stick together. To my brothers, Ben and John, and my sister-in-law Bev, thank you for looking out for me when I needed it most, and for being my family even when I was probably at peak annoying.

To Margaret, thank you for holding my hand the whole way through. Thanks to Erin Gray for always bringing the peace. A special shout-out to my girlies, Sydney, Sophie, Mia, and Ollie, for always bringing the laughter. And to attorney extraordinaire Stephanie Murphy, who fearlessly advocated for my dad, even after his death.

And a chef's kiss to Biz Evans and her Brown Fox Coffee in Mount Pleasant, South Carolina, for reminding me that there is nothing in life so bad that a cold brew at the Fox can't cure. Y'all should try it sometime! Truth.

ABOUT THE AUTHOR

Eva Benefield is a true-crime survivor, an influencer, the CEO of OrphanTok, a marathon runner, a surfer, a sourdough specialist, a coffee connoisseur, an animal lover, and a collector of shark's teeth, peak moments, and great friends. Eva is also an artist and designer, and the founder of her own apparel company, Ghost Cowboy, based in her hometown of Charleston, South Carolina.